T0191395

THE COLLABORATION BOOK

MIKAEL KROGERUS
ROMAN TSCHÄPPELER

THE COLLABORATION BOOK

A GUIDE TO ACHIEVING GREAT THINGS TOGETHER

Translated from the German by Gesche Ipsen

W. W. NORTON & COMPANY

Independent Publishers Since 1923

First published in Great Britain in 2024 by Profile Books as
The Collaboration Book: 41 Ideas for Working Better Together
First published in 2022 in Switzerland by Kein & Aber AG Zurich

All rights reserved
Printed in the United States of America
First American Edition 2024

For information about permission to reproduce selections from this book,
write to Permissions, W. W. Norton & Company, Inc., 500 Fifth Avenue,
New York, NY 10110

For information about special discounts for bulk purchases, please
contact W. W. Norton Special Sales at specialsales@wwnorton.com
or 800-233-4830

Manufacturing by Versa Press

ISBN 978-1-324-07537-0

W. W. Norton & Company, Inc.
500 Fifth Avenue, New York, N.Y. 10110
www.wwnorton.com

W. W. Norton & Company Ltd.
15 Carlisle Street, London W1D 3BS

1 2 3 4 5 6 7 8 9 0

CONTENTS

FOREWORD:
SMELLS LIKE
TEAM SPIRIT

This book was written and illustrated by two friends who love nothing more than working together. It all started over twenty years ago, in Denmark, at the Aarhus-based Kaospilot school for creative leadership and meaningful entrepreneurship – which has been described as a Rudolf Steiner school for grown-ups, or a sort of "creative" MBA.

Two things in particular have stayed with us from our student days:
1. There is your goal, and then there's how you achieve it. Kaospilot's mantra was that the outcome of a project matters less than understanding how you got there.
2. There is no "I" in "team."

The latter is easy to dismiss as merely one of those typical clichéd slogans, but it is worth taking seriously. After all, isn't it true that we rarely achieve anything on our own? If you look closely, everything humanity has ever created is the result of a collaborative process. We hardly ever truly achieve something alone – and even when we do, it's only because other people have made it possible. Perhaps they paved the way for us, or provided their support; or perhaps, with them by our side, we were able to become a better version of ourselves.

Even solo climbers and solo violinists don't really work solo. They too need a team who supports, coaches and looks after them. Even if you can't afford an entourage, you still need someone to take care of the kids while you train or practice, someone who gives you a hug when you're down.

This is one of the lessons that reproductive labor can teach productive labor. The productive sector – where, in return for pay, workers create goods and services with a monetary value – is based on competition, guided by the belief that the best will emerge the winner. Meanwhile, the reproductive sector – unpaid domestic work, caring for others, cultivating relationships – is based on collaboration, and we instinctively understand that there are no winners. Rather, if we want to make sure that no one loses out, we have to work together. This idea is beginning to percolate into the private business sector too. Individual (and, as a rule, male) genius may still be idealized, but almost all sectors now expect you to be a team player. "Maverick" or "lone wolf" are words you'll rarely see mentioned in a job posting.

Being able to work well with others is a requirement for almost every job, but no one ever teaches us how to do it. Crazy as it might be, people assume that it's something you are either born with or simply acquire as you go along – or not, as the case may be. In truth, though, collaboration isn't a character trait, it's a skill.

For this book, we searched for answers to forty-four questions related to collaboration, such as: How can a group of people reach a decision, when everyone disagrees with each other? How big should a team ideally be? Naturally, teamwork also has certain downsides – sorry: poses certain challenges. Who takes the blame when a project fails? What do you do when someone is being a real pain? How does relationship management work in a team?

Here, we focus on three areas that require your constant attention.

Solving Problems
Let's not pretend: every team, no matter how well it functions, will sooner or later face obstacles, dissent or failure. There is no such thing as a team that never runs into difficulties. What distinguishes good teams from bad ones, however, is that good teams find ways to overcome problems.

Achieving Your Goals
A team is a marriage of convenience. You have come together to achieve something you can't achieve on your own. What connects you is the goal. As everyone knows, there's more than one way to skin a cat.

Creating Trust
Two or more people in the same room don't necessarily constitute a team. They have to coalesce first, find a common cause and a common language, and get themselves organized. Trust is key.

Writing and illustrating this book has changed us. Anything you work long and hard on changes you. And it wasn't that we became grandmasters in collaboration overnight; it was more like learning a new language. We hope that you'll feel the same way after reading our book. However, don't think of it as a strict template: approach it more like a small toolkit to keep handy at work. Try this or that, find out what works for you, and don't worry about the rest. And most importantly, look forward to working with your team.

Roman Tschäppeler   Mikael Krogerus

THE SACRED TRIANGLE OF TEAMS

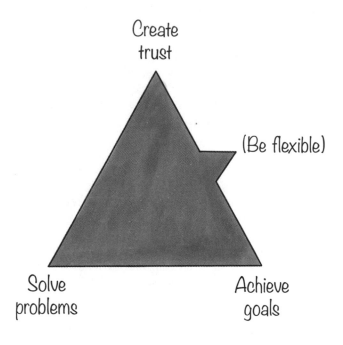

Create
trust

(Be flexible)

Solve
problems

Achieve
goals

Solve problems (p. 5), achieve your goals (p. 69) and create trust (p. 115).

Solving Problems

THE TWO-PIZZA RULE: HOW BIG SHOULD YOUR TEAM BE?

Thomas Widmer, the famous Swiss hiker, was once asked about the ideal size of a hiking group. His answer was: "Six people max, or you'll run into problems. If you have eleven people traipsing into an inn, the landlord will have a coronary."

Widmer probably wasn't aware that his words echoed Jeff Bezos's "two-pizza rule." Bezos came up with the rule not long after founding Amazon, and the company still swears by it today: a team should be small enough that it can be fed by two pizzas. Two pizzas feed roughly four to seven people. If you follow the two-pizza rule, you'll be able to incorporate very different characters in your team (see illustration), thus gaining a diversity of ideas and perspectives while keeping things manageable and flexible. In small groups, people can't hide behind anonymity or indifference, so everyone takes a greater share of the responsibility. There will also be fewer political shenanigans, because there aren't enough people to forge secondary alliances. Finally, small groups make it easier to turn strangers into friends – since everyone has to interact with everyone else at some point.

According to occupational psychologist J. Richard Hackman, moderately sized teams also have the advantage that they make communication easier: the bigger the team, the more opinions there are, the longer the meetings and the greater the dissent will be, which slows the whole decision-making process down. Too many chefs spoil the pizza.

Of course, the two-pizza rule doesn't work everywhere. A philharmonic orchestra can't consist of four people, otherwise it would be a quartet; and a baseball team by definition has to have nine players players. However, it does work in a surprisingly large number of situations.

So the first question to ask when a team isn't working as it should is: how big is it?

If you need more than two

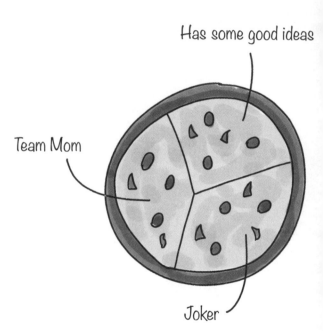

Has some good ideas

Team Mom

Joker

Good teams musn't be too big, and should have the right ingredients.

as to feed your team, it's too big

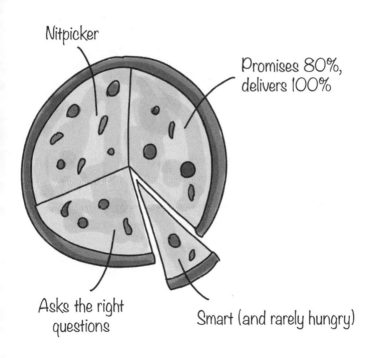

Nitpicker

Promises 80%, delivers 100%

Asks the right questions

Smart (and rarely hungry)

TUCKMAN'S STAGES: HOW A GROUP BECOMES A TEAM

Teamwork is a rollercoaster ride. A team's mood will go up and down, as will its team spirit and, needless to say, its output. At times you want to squeal with joy; at others you almost feel like throwing up. During the ride, you regret ever having got on, but as soon as it stops you're desperate to get back on (or tell yourself: "Never again").

Yet not all teams are the same.

We often react passively, even to the atmosphere in a group: our attitude is that things either work or they don't – it's a question of luck, that's all, and there's nothing we can do about it. However, studies have shown that teams aren't a lottery. You have to work at them. They don't simply come together: turning a loose array of people into a strong team is a process. In the 1960s, psychologist Bruce Tuckman came up with the following model for the typical stages of group development:

Forming

The group comes together. Getting to know each other is often underscored by a sense of insecurity. What will the others think of me? Will they accept me? What role will I play? During this phase, the relationship between the various team members is still completely undefined and unclear. They don't trust each other yet.

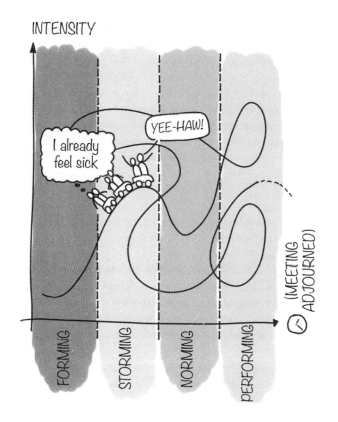

Storming

Following the first stage of uncertainty, everyone in the team finds their role. Some actively take it on, others have it assigned to them. During this stage, you constantly need to balance your own interests with those of the group. There will be power struggles and other conflicts. Be warned: some teams never make it past this stage.

Norming

As the team members resolve any remaining disagreements, start thinking about their shared goal, agree on the rules and core values, and work together to define the various roles, their confidence automatically grows and everyone feels motivated.

Performing

Now the real work can begin.

Adjourning

The team members say goodbye to each other and their common endeavor. Ideally, they will reflect together on their experience working as a team, and learn some useful things for next time. Occasionally, teams will find themselves in the adjournment phase before the project has even ended.

Although Tuckman's model has become a popular way to describe team development, it does have its critics. First among them was Tuckman himself. He believed that his model "cannot be considered truly representative of small-group developmental processes [...] rather, it must serve as stimulus for further research." Furthermore, he observed these stages not in work settings but in therapy groups. Now, you might look at a team and say, yes, it definitely displays some pathological traits – but still, proceed with care.

In 2007, Kate Cassidy re-evaluated Tuckman's work and concluded that although the stages are essentially right, the line between them is blurred. There's a certain amount of overlap and repetition – and conflict can occur in all phases, not just the "storming" one. Ah well. Still, it's worth showing Tuckman's model to your team before they start on a project, and to regularly ask the team members:

a. "How far along are we with the project?" (i.e. which stage you're at), and
b. "What do we need to get to the next stage?"

One final suggestion: people frequently think that good teams never experience tension, but in fact the opposite is true. Good teams merely understand that tension isn't a problem – rather, it's an opportunity to put your heads together to find a solution. Therefore, don't shy away from uncomfortable conversations; and when conflict arises, be transparent. One thing to remember is to make sure you distinguish between relationship conflicts and task conflicts. Relationship conflicts – me versus you – are about a clash of personalities. They are usually unproductive and draining. Task conflicts, meanwhile – my idea versus yours – can promote creativity and enjoyment.

RUN THE BANK VERSUS CHANGE THE BANK: ARE YOU A VISIONARY OR A CREATOR?

In most companies, project teams and committees, you will find two factions: one that always wants to change something, and one that wants to keep the status quo. While the first is thinking about the day after tomorrow, the second is thinking about the day-to-day business. The first wants to evolve, the second wants to preserve and manage.

In the corporate world, these divergent attitudes are called "change the bank" and "run the bank."

The friction between the two factions can have various causes. Perhaps the "changers" are making decisions that negatively affect the "runners," or have bold ideas but aren't interested in how they're implemented. Conversely, changers often regard runners as chronic naysayers (see *Saying No*, p. 112) and albatrosses round their necks. Then again, changers are usually more highly regarded than runners – someone who suggests a different way of doing the dishes is respected more than the person who does the dishes every day.

Of course, we need both people who come up with new ideas and people who carry them out. But how can we ease the tension between the two camps?

People involved in IT have given this matter a lot of thought. One solution they've come up with is DevOps teams, a contraction of the terms "development" and "operations." The theory is that when developers and programmers work together, there is less friction and greater mutual understanding. The DevOps mantra is: "You built it, you run it." When someone has an idea, they should be the one to implement and maintain it. People who take the initiative are respected, but they also have to accept responsibility for what they do. In other words, you should bear the consequences of your decisions. Why is that?

In large corporations, the changers often don't find out the result of their decisions, because several office floors and many months lie between the idea and its execution. The further we are from the results of our decisions, the easier it is to convince ourselves that we are right. At the micro level, though, you can see the immediate results.

DevOps teams are an attempt to combine the micro and macro levels. The thinking behind this is that if changers are made to execute their own ideas, they'll inevitably acquire a better understanding of the challenges their implementation presents. At the same time, the runners will discover that not every change is a threat.

DevOps doesn't mean that everyone has to do everything. It doesn't mean saying goodbye to the division of labor. All it means is that change and implementation go hand in hand, and that there is no theory without practice, no creator without a client.

When visionaries and creators collide, trouble ensues – or it might generate some great ideas.

I CAN DO IT

$$x = \frac{-b \pm \sqrt{b^2 - 4ac}}{2a}$$

HYBRID WORK: WHAT'S BETTER – WFH OR WFO?

The Covid pandemic has revealed an interesting fact about office life: many staff prefer to work from home – but managers like to have them in the office.

But which is better?

Both are.

Microsoft once conducted an investigation which showed that WFH is usually fine for existing teams, where everyone knows each other and is familiar with the processes, company culture and expectations. The problem, however, is the company's future: when people work remotely, relationships stagnate, and work becomes static and isolated. You end up with a silo mentality, which is bad for innovation – and really bad when it comes to onboarding new recruits.

The solution is a combination of WFH and WFO – working from home *and* working from the office. You can already see it happening in lots of companies, but what is the best way to deal with it? By way of an answer, Gartner, the consulting firm, suggests you ask these two questions: does everyone have to be in the same **place** when they work, and does everyone have to work at the same **time**?

Here is a matrix that shows four different working styles:

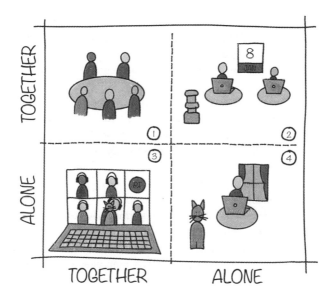

Knowing when to work with others and when to work alone is a useful skill to have.

Together together
Teams meet physically in the same place. Meetings, workshops and kick-off sessions are key to creating collective experiences and memories. For new staff, they are crucial for networking and familiarizing themselves with the corporate culture.

Together alone
The teams are in the same place, but everyone works on their own. This means that they can focus on "deep work," i.e. immerse themselves in one thing, without interruptions. At the same time, though, interactions with other people are definitely allowed, because you can't do deep work for ever. To facilitate both focused work and interaction between colleagues, office planners and interior designers have to think differently. What if we put an end to open-plan offices, and reintroduced doors?

Alone together
Teams work in different places, e.g. from home, but are connected virtually. Ah yes, the good old Zoom meeting. But here too we should open ourselves up to new possibilities: maybe not everyone needs to sit at home in front of a laptop in their pyjama bottoms – why not walk your dog during meetings, or hit the treadmill? One advantage of being physically in motion during meetings is that you won't be able to send emails or check social media at the same time, meaning that you'll pay more attention. (But don't do anything that will distract the other people on the call; turn the camera off if necessary. And always use the mute button.)

Alone alone
Teams work remotely and in shifts. If someone likes to start work early, they can, and if someone prefers to work through

the night, that's fine too. That way, everyone can get down to deep work whenever they like. To facilitate this way of working, though, we need to consider no-meeting days, no-message days and offline hours.

NEW PAY: THE SALARY OF THE FUTURE

Here's a little thought experiment: imagine you've been invited to come up with a salary structure for the whole world – on the condition that you don't know where on the scale your own salary will fall. What will you suggest?

Philosopher John Rawls called this the "veil of ignorance." In our particular case, the veil in question is that you don't know what your place in the hierarchy would be. If you don't know whether your own position would be advantageous, you'll propose an equitable system.

In reality, when the topic is salaries, most companies are unwilling to go in for fairness. New work? Yes, please. New pay? No, thanks.

Here's a brief glossary:
Old pay: staff salaries are negotiated individually.
New pay: a salary scheme that everyone agrees is fair.

The old pay structures benefit people who are very confident, good at negotiating and male. New pay structures try to avoid this by employing different salary models:
1. *Universal*: everyone is paid the same.
2. *Need-based*: everyone earns what they need, depending on their circumstances.
3. *Modular*: maybe everyone who does the same job earns the same; or all junior staff earn one salary, and all senior

staff earn another; or everyone gets a raise once every five years.

4. *Proportional*: the top salary paid by the company is no more than (e.g.) four times the lowest.
5. *Team-based*: everyone who works in the same team earns the same.
6. *Self-determined*: everyone decides how much they earn.

The last one may sound particularly silly, but a study has shown that when people are allowed to set their own salary, they might earn more (obviously) – but they'll also increase the company's profits (ta-da!).

There are two essential conditions when it comes to new pay. First, it must be equitable. People think it's unfair when they are underpaid, but, interestingly, they also don't like being overpaid. The easiest thing to do here is orientate yourself on the salary market; if your competitors all pay more, even the fairest new pay scheme is no use. Second, the process has to be transparent. This doesn't mean that everyone should know what their colleagues earn, but that everyone should know how compensation is determined. Only then will they trust the system – and each other.

An overview of different kinds of salary structures.

RED TEAM VERSUS BLUE TEAM: HOW TO AVOID GROUPTHINK

We all at some point come across an *advocatus diaboli* – a devil's advocate. They are notorious spoilsports, and you can find them in every meeting. As a rule, they only raise counter-arguments for argument's sake. They nitpick, talk at cross-purposes, find fault and talk things down, by turns being a frustrating and entertaining old grumpy boots. Their objections are occasionally reasonable, but more often are merely an expression of their character rather than a constructive contribution to the decision-making process.

They are an irritant, but have historically played an important role. Ever since the sixteenth century, whenever the Roman Catholic Church considers whether to canonize someone, a God's advocate (Latin: *advocatus dei*) will argue their case while a devil's advocate regards the candidate's character with skepticism. The latter's job is not to talk the candidate down, but – because the decision is an important one – to uncover any blind spots or errors in logic.

Whoever comes up with a plan is naturally very much in favor of it. A team, let's call it the Blue Team, will have spent days, weeks or even months on it, and is convinced that they have taken all eventualities into account. Casting a critical eye over their own work becomes harder and harder the further along they are in the planning, and the more fully they have developed their ideas – because any reservations raised late on in the process could torpedo the entire project.

That's where the Red Team comes in, whose task is to play devil's advocate.

They interrogate everything. Literally everything.

First principles, the people who came up with the plan, their motive, the status quo.

They interrogate everyone. Literally everyone.

Groupthink poses the biggest danger of all. The boss or expert says A, and everyone else nods, including those who actually think B, because they're worried they'll make fools of themselves, or delay the process unnecessarily. The Red Team disrupts this groupthink by questioning each individual member of the team. Do they have any concerns, further thoughts, alternative proposals?

So next time you find yourself listening to a big new insight or strategy announcement, ask yourself: "Has it been red-teamed yet?"

Get a second opinion. It won't necessarily be right, but it'll reveal how solid the first one is.

AGILITY: HOW MUCH FREEDOM DO TEAM MEMBERS NEED?

Those among us who started working before the turn of the millennium are more than familiar with the world of SSEE: stable, secure, easy, explicit. Then, overnight, the digital VUCA world arrived: volatile, uncertain, complex and ambiguous.

"Agility" is a way to get organized in a VUCA world. All sorts of interesting principles and clever techniques are associated with it. Here, we'll focus on two aspects, which agility pioneer Henrik Kniberg described as follows: staff should have a great degree of **autonomy** when it comes to decision-making. But they also need clear **direction** in the shape of goals, visions and guidelines, to ensure that everyone is working toward the same end.

1. **Little direction, little autonomy**
   Management tells staff what to do, but not *why* it needs to be done.
2. **Lots of direction, little autonomy**
   Management tells staff what needs to be done and why, but also *how* to do it.
3. **Little direction, lots of autonomy**
   Management lets everyone do as they please.
4. **Lots of direction, lots of autonomy**
   Management tells staff what needs to be done and why, but lets the team decide *how* to achieve it.

Number 4 is agile work.

Leading people means allowing them some freedom. Being led means being able to handle that freedom.

INTEGRATIVE DECISION-MAKING: HOW TO MAKE DECISIONS AS A TEAM

Having to make a decision as a team, rather than solo, is one of the most common as well as one of the trickiest moments in anyone's working life.

The two most common ways to come to a decision are "top down" (i.e. the boss decides) and "bottom up" (i.e. the democratic way, where the team members vote and the majority rules).

Unfortunately, neither method is ideal. The first excludes the most important stakeholders of all, the team members; the second means that up to 49 percent of the team disagrees with the decision.

There is another way to do it: the integrative decision-making approach. The name might be a bit odd, but we know it as a reliable way of achieving your goal – if you follow all the steps properly, and have someone there to moderate the process:

1. Describe the problem
The person wanting to make the decision briefly explains their starting point, i.e. the problem – or "challenge," as some prefer to call it.

For example, a member of staff working in a large bakery believes that gluten is bad for both us and the environment, and that it's high time that producers working with wheat do something about it.

AUTOCRACY
The boss decides

DEMOCRACY
The majority decides

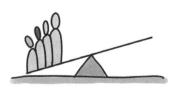

INTEGRATIVE
DECISION-MAKING
We decide

2. Suggest something

Next, that person makes a suggestion, which should be as concrete as possible. It's not about finding the perfect solution for all time, but about kicking things off by putting an idea out there.

The member of staff suggests that the bakery should stop selling wheat products.

3. Ask useful questions

Now, everyone should start asking questions that will help clarify the proposal. The key thing is to ask questions that "gather information" rather than dispense it.

"Do we know for sure that wheat is bad for us and the environment?"

4. First reactions

Next, everyone says what they think of the suggestion. They can say whatever they like, so long as it isn't insulting.

"I think that's a great idea," or "I don't think it's a good idea."

5. Explain and adjust

It's the proposer's turn again. They should explain more clearly what they mean, and take the opportunity to adjust or refine their proposal based on any objections that have been raised.

6. Objections

Each team member has another chance to voice their opinion. If they have an objection, they should raise it.

"I worry that what you suggest could be harmful, and there won't be any way to fix it."

"If we stop selling wheat products, we'll go bankrupt."

7. Integration

The moderator asks how the suggestion could be tweaked further, to address the concerns that have been raised – while still at least partially solving the original problem. Address each objection in turn, not at the same time.

"How about introducing a no-wheat day?"

You'll then end up with something that might not be *exactly* what the proposer wanted, but to which no one objects.

In other words, you are looking not for an idea to which everyone says yes, but an idea to which no one says no (see *Consensus versus Consent*, p. 94).

PSYCHOLOGICAL SAFETY: IF YOU NEED TO BE BOLD, YOU HAVE TO FEEL SAFE

Why do we feel comfortable in some groups but insecure in others? And how important is feeling comfortable when it comes to performance?

The answer to the second question is: very. It's the most important factor of all.

The first question is harder to answer.

We all know how it is. In the company of some people, we're cheerful, generous and self-confident; with others, we're more negative, envious, taciturn. It's almost as if there are two completely different personalities inside us, which are so diametrically opposed as to seem alien to each other. The obvious answer is that we simply have good days and bad days. Which is true. And also isn't. In reality, our behavior is frequently affected by those around us. In 1999, behaviorist Amy Edmondson published a much-talked-about article in which she described feeling comfortable in a group setting as "psychological safety."

She explains the concept using two parameters: How safe do I feel in the group, and how well am I performing?

If you feel insecure and are underperforming, you've mentally given up. You're in the "apathy zone."

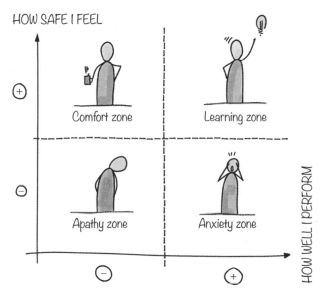

If you feel insecure but are performing well, you are in the "anxiety zone."

If you feel safe and perform badly, you are in the "comfort zone."

If you feel safe and perform well, you are in the "learning zone."

When you're the learning zone, you'll be bold enough to admit to the team that you don't understand something, bold enough to suggest crazy or half-thought-out ideas, bold enough to admit mistakes, and bold enough to point out other people's mistakes. It's the only way to learn – hence the name.

It's as obvious as it is true that when people feel safe they're more cheerful, friendly, inspired, empathetic and courageous; and when they feel insecure they're more hesitant, egotistical, boring and skeptical. This last point is especially worth noting: when we feel insecure, we tend to see the negative in everything, and are less accepting of new suggestions or other people. Our negativity and skepticism then make those around us more defensive.

Yet psychological safety is not to be confused with fake smiles, forced optimism or constant praise. It doesn't mean that everything necessarily has to be nice and pleasant. It means feeling safe enough – whether at the office, with your colleagues or among family – to address mistakes without having to worry about endangering relationships. It means being able to criticize someone's idea without having to worry that they will be offended and snap at you.

Psychological safety starts with you. We all tend to hide our weaknesses and highlight our strengths – and that's fine. However, it doesn't help create an environment of psychological safety. To do that, we need to be open about our insecurities, about the things we don't know and about what we owe to others. The three most important sentences to say in a group setting if you want to create a sense of psychological safety are:

- What do you think?
- I was wrong.
- Thank you for doing that.

THE LADDER OF INFERENCE: HOW TO SOLVE TEAM CONFLICTS

Think back to a time when you came into conflict with a colleague or boss. How certain are you that your assessment of the situation, or of the other person, was correct?

Often, what an argument is about isn't the same as why the argument occurs in the first place. This is the central tenet of Harvard professor Chris Argyris's "ladder of inference," which is a great way to unravel a conflict and start talking about the real issue.

Let's take a closer look at the ladder. It has seven rungs:

1. **Observation.** You register what someone says or does.
2. **Filtering.** However, you don't register everything, only part of it. Based on past experience and the mood you're in, you'll blank out most of the situation and instead focus on what you subconsciously think matters.
3. **Interpretation.** You assess the situation, develop a theory about it and make assumptions.
4. **Judgment.** You construct a narrative about the events.
5. **Deduction.** You come to a conclusion.
6. **Reassurance.** You convince yourself that your thinking is correct.
7. **Action.** You do something.

Here's a well-known anecdote to illustrate how easy it is to make false assumptions. You want to visit a friend in the hospital, and are looking for a parking space. There's one over there! You're about to park, when suddenly another car comes steaming along and pulls into it. You think: "What a jerk!," roll down the window and get ready to launch a tirade at them. But then the driver comes up to apologize – they've just had a call to say that their partner has gone into labor, and are in a rush to get to her.

Now you see the situation differently, and feel bad for having jumped to conclusions.

This example is perhaps slightly extreme – proper conflicts usually don't arise from small misunderstandings, but from actual slights. But in those cases, too, you should ask yourself: do you really know why the other person is angry? Or, conversely, does the person you're upset with know what it's actually all about?

Conflicts can only be resolved if each party knows where the other one is coming from. Therefore, whenever we assume something about someone, we should ask them whether our assumption is correct.

It sounds ridiculous – until you try it.

What I think our problem is

The most important communication rule of all is: ask.

<u>What the actual problem is –</u>
<u>now that I've asked you</u>

ASSUME POSITIVE INTENT: HOW TO DEAL WITH (PRESUMED) IDIOTS

Are you up for an experiment?

For the next twenty-four hours, assume that everyone around you means well.

The woman who pushes in front of you on the train? That relative of yours who's refusing to get vaccinated? The guy who sent you a rude email? The colleague who showed you up in the meeting? For the next twenty-four hours, assume that none of them are intentionally trying to annoy or hurt you. In other words, give everyone you meet today the benefit of the doubt.

Why? Because most of the time, when someone lets their bad mood out on you or acts arrogantly toward you, it isn't actually about *you*. They are the way they are today for any number of reasons: maybe they slept badly, maybe they've been arguing with their partner, maybe they're just insecure and trying to hide it. You can't change them – but you can change your attitude toward them. When it comes to communication, you reap what you sow: most people answer mistrust with mistrust, but they'll also answer a smile with a smile. As the comedian Ricky Gervais once said: "The only shortcut that works [is] kindness."

We won't pretend that it isn't a tough ask.

Everyone has that movie playing in their head, showing all the (bad) things people say about you, how unfair the world is, how mean others are to you. This is called "negativity bias," whereby a single negative comment affects us more than ten compliments. But although negative things may affect us more, remember that positive things are more common.

This technique is called "assume positive intent" (API).

It's easy to make fun of it. We all have examples of when we were right, after all, when our initial skepticism proved justified.

Despite that – or perhaps precisely because of it – why not give API a try?

What people say about me

You're good. You're no good. You're good. You're good. You're good. You're good. You're good. You're good. You're good. You're good. You're good. You're good. You're good. You're good. You're good.

Negativity bias means focusing on the negative, even when people praise you. Which is a shame.

<u>What I hear</u>

You're no good.

THE BAD APPLE EXPERIMENT: WHAT TO DO WHEN SOMEONE IN THE TEAM ANNOYS YOU

We've all come across bad apples: that annoying person in the group, the grouch in the meeting, who spoils the team's mood with their derogatory comments and destructive opinions.

How powerful are bad apples – and how do you deal with them?

Will Felps decided to find out. In 2006, this professor at the Rotterdam School of Management conducted an experiment in which he divided students into groups of four, and gave them forty-five minutes to solve a task. What the guinea pigs didn't know was that, in some groups, one member was an actor playing one of these three destructive personality types:

The pessimist, who complains that the task is no fun and expresses their doubt as to the group's ability to complete it.
The jerk, who constantly critiques with other people's ideas, but never comes up with any useful suggestions themselves.
The slacker, who announces right at the start that they can't be bothered and just goofs off in their chair.

At the time, the prevailing thinking was that groups dominate individuals, rather than the other way round, and there were tons of studies showing that individuals tend to adopt the norms and values of whatever group they're in.

☐ IGNORE THEM?

☐ CONFRONT THEM?

☐ EMBRACE THEM?

What do you do when the idiot in your team trashes your ideas yet again?

But Felps discovered that the opposite is true.

The groups that included an actor – i.e. a bad apple – on average performed 30–40 percent worse than the others. More than that: the three "genuine" team members were observed to take on the actor's characteristics. If the actor pretended to be a jerk, the others acted like jerks too; when they pretended to be lazy, the other members became less ambitious too. The results seemed clear-cut: the most annoying member of a group has the biggest effect on team performance, and no group is immune.

Actually, not quite. One team remained unimpressed. The actor was unable to change the mood – on the contrary, the other members changed *them*, to the extent that they broke character and started cooperating. At first, it didn't look as if anything special had occurred. But as it turned out, when the actor started complaining, one of the other three, with an open smile, asked the other two what they thought of the actor's suggestion.

That person had a gift. They were a born leader. But what exactly did they do?

1. With their positive, disarming body language, they signaled to the group that the person wasn't a threat. Which was true. The real danger was that they would infect the rest of the group with their negative attitude. Solution: react to the bad apple's criticism as if they had just proposed that everyone turns up at tomorrow's meeting in a bikini. Smile, and ask, curiously: "Sure, but why?" That way, you're showing the others that what you're dealing with is harmless, if interesting. Embrace the bad apple.

2. The next thing they did was to invite the group to discuss the proposal. Even annoying people sometimes make a

valid point. But make sure you do it in a positive environment, otherwise you'll end up wasting your energy.

In conclusion: irritants are contagious, so if someone behaves like a jerk, others will start behaving like jerks too. They also waste everyone's time, because they force you to deal with them, rather than with the task in hand.

But they are human too, and if they can affect our behavior, the reverse is also true. When someone smiles at them, they find it hard not to smile back.

THE RECIPROCITY RING: LEARNING TO ASK FOR HELP

Years ago, while studying at the Kaospilot business school in Denmark, we learnt a technique that makes it easier to ask for help. It's called the "reciprocity ring," developed by entrepreneur Cheryl Baker and sociologist Wayne Baker.

The participants each come up with something they want, be it work-related or purely personal, but which they need help to get. For instance: "I'd like to work for Google someday," or "I'm looking for an apartment with a patio," or "I'd like to go to the Beyoncé show, but it's sold out," or "I'm looking for a cheaper way to install solar panels on my roof." Next, everyone is asked to use their knowledge and contacts to help others achieve their goal.

At the time, we thought, well, all right, why not? But what happened next was quite extraordinary: everyone really pulled out all the stops to help, both the students who already knew each other, and those who didn't know each other from Adam. Strikingly, we did so even for fellow students we didn't particularly like. Evidently, people get a lot of pleasure out of solving other people's problems. You'll find an astonishing wealth of resources within a given group of people – in other words, other people can be wonderfully helpful when you're stuck.

The reciprocity ring works for everyone, in any context. At work, a reciprocity ring can help refresh the relationship between long-standing colleagues; or you could create one

that includes people from different departments, who you think might be helpful to each other in some way. Or you could create a small circle among your close friends, to help each other with domestic or personal issues.

The key takeaway from this is that helping others and letting others help you results in close and lasting relationships. When you lend someone a hand, you like them more. This is a perfectly normal psychological reaction – we justify our actions by telling ourselves that we have helped someone out because we actually like them.

Wayne Baker raises a fascinating paradox here: the problem isn't that people aren't willing to help, but that many of us are reluctant to ask. The underlying reason for our hesitation may be that we don't rightly know how to do it, or are afraid to admit that we need help, lest others think us weak or stupid. Interestingly, the opposite is true: when someone asks for help, the people around them normally perceive them as competent. Sometimes, too, the reason we don't ask for help is that we underestimate other people's willingness or ability to do so.

How do we get over our reluctance?

You might think that real reciprocity starts with someone selflessly offering to help. Not so. Reciprocity starts with someone asking for it.

So if you want to establish a culture of mutual support in your team, you don't need generous people who constantly assist others in their endeavors. You need to create a climate where it's normal and OK to ask for help.

RADICAL CANDOR: HOW TO GIVE FEEDBACK WITHIN A GROUP

In her book *Radical Candor*, Kim Scott uses a matrix to explain how to approach feedback without qualms. Her matrix has two axes (see illustration).

Challenge directly
You can provide feedback either in a vague, generalizing way ("You're ruining the atmosphere with your behavior") or concretely and directly ("What you said just now has ruined the atmosphere in the team, because you said ... when it might have been better if you'd said ..."). Vague and abstract feedback is easy. Concrete feedback, where you pinpoint the problem and name it, requires effort.

Care personally
You can be ruthless in your feedback, and not spare a thought for how the other person feels; or you can approach feedback as if giving it to your best friend: firmly, but kindly, not from self-interest but out of consideration for the other person.

The matrix thus creates four kinds of feedback:

Manipulative insincerity
You're neither concrete nor convey the sense that the person you're talking to matters. Such feedback is unconstructive and hurtful.

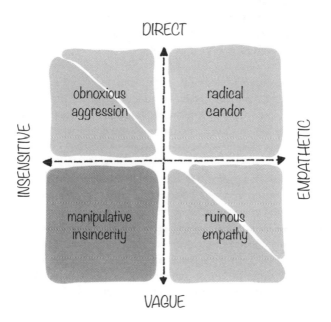

Obnoxious aggression
Feedback that's personal, direct and ruthless. You take aim at the issue, but don't care if you end up injuring the person you're talking to.

Ruinous empathy
For whatever reason, you're reluctant to be honest, and wrap your criticism in praise. The other person is important to you, so you lie to them.

Radical candor
You are utterly honest, but also really care about the feelings of your interlocutor. This kind of feedback focuses on what the other person can do better next time, not on what they did wrong this time.

This theory suggests that honesty is always the best policy, but there are instances when it can also be harmful, when it would be wiser to keep your criticisms to yourself or express them more subtly. It's often a cultural thing: what Germans consider friendly honesty can be considered insulting in the US. Or it might be a question of your relationship with the other person, or the other person's character. A little piece of advice: before you criticize someone, briefly ask yourself how you would react if someone said the same thing to you.

There's another dimension to the feedback question in group contexts: should critique be expressed one-to-one, or in front of everyone else? Kim Scott believes the former: praise in public, criticize in private. But Pascal Grieder, former CEO of the telecommunications firm Salt, thinks the latter:

Transparency is important to me, so I always express my criticism in front of the rest of the team, rather than one-to-one. It works the other way round as well: I totally respect people who tell their boss when they disagree with something, and do it in front of the whole team.

It clearly depends on the situation and the people involved, their personalities and preferences. Grieder's approach might be worth considering: by giving feedback in front of the whole group you'll increase transparency and thus the sense of trust within the team. Even then, Scott's tips for giving feedback should be kept in mind. Ask yourself: Am I showing that I care personally? Am I challenging directly?

4-IN-1 PERSPECTIVE: WHAT COLLABORATION MEANS FOR SOCIETY

In a podcast, author Teresa Bücker once asked a question that everyone should ask themselves at some point: who would I be, if I didn't have a job?

It's worth thinking about. You could be laid off or get sick, or your particular field of work could become obsolete. Who are you, without your job? Will you still like yourself if you're no longer successful? To put it differently: what, beyond work, makes you who you are?

Bücker says that we tend to overly identify with our jobs. We are under so much pressure to work hard that the line between our working lives and leisure time has become blurred, and the two often overlap. When you open your laptop at 11 p.m., it often isn't clear whether you're working, networking, relaxing or none of the above.

A few years ago, sociologist Frigga Haug proposed an interesting alternative. Her idea of the "4-in-1 perspective" suggests that life has four dimensions, to which we should allocate an equal proportion of a sixteen-hour day (since we sleep on average eight hours a day):

1. Earning a living: working for money; it's what we usually call our "job."
2. Care work: domestic and family matters, as well as cultivating friendships and romantic relationships.

3. Cultural self-realization: art, spirituality, exercise, etc.; these are important to our personal development, so shouldn't be treated like a rare luxury.
4. Engagement: a living society needs engaged citizens; it doesn't mean that you should become a politician, but there are other ways to contribute: get involved in your community, or in a club or association, or get involved with social issues.

A moment's thought shows how far-reaching this model could prove. Curtailing our working lives to four hours a day would give more people access to paid employment – part-time jobs for all. But also caring jobs for all. Self-realization for all. Social engagement for all. Some people would end up having less money, but for that they'd have more of other things. Others would have more of everything.

TODAY

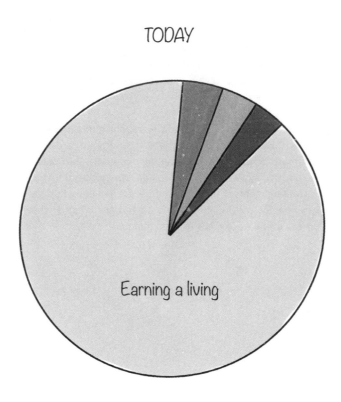

Social teamwork means that everyone does less of one thing and more of everything else.

PROPOSAL

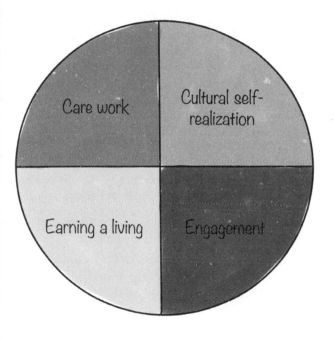

BURNOUT: SPEND MORE TIME MESSING ABOUT

Let's talk about burnout for a moment. Not the full-blown clinical version, but its preamble: exhaustion, the feeling that you can't – and don't want to – do this anymore, that you're no longer up to it. If we're being honest, we all know the feeling.

One aspect of the problem is a question that's surprisingly little talked about at work: how do I deal with pressure?

Pressure is not a bad thing in itself. Many like it when a deadline looms or when three things all come at once, because it's only then that they really get going. But in the long run, pressure leads you into a dead end. You keep going until you can't – and then keep going some more.

There is simply no end to it, no end-of-play, no conclusion. You feel like your whole life is a to-do list, where you somehow have to tick off, one by one, all the annoying things as well as the nice ones; the list seems endless, and ticks are in charge. You're about to burn out.

It's easy to say: "Take a break, slow down." We would, if we could!

Most of the time, the pressure comes from above – we *have* to do certain things. Often, it comes from outside – we think we have to *be* a certain way. And even when it comes from within ourselves, when we put ourselves under pressure, you can't simply turn it off with a flip of a switch.

If you want to deal better with all that pressure and shield yourself from burnout, this is what you should do: create little windows of time for silliness and goofing off.

It makes sense, doesn't it? Make time in your schedule for messing around. For games. For doodling. For talking about nothing. Even for an inappropriately early after-work drink. This means setting aside (an) hour(s) to scroll through Insta – which you don't think of as wasted time, but as much-needed playtime.

Focusing entirely on work without pause won't make you more productive. It will lead to burnout. Messing about for a while won't interfere with your work; rather, it's a way to rediscover the joy of work.

Achieving Your Goals

SMALL WINS: HOW TO APPROACH IMPOSSIBLE TASKS

All teams sooner or later hit a wall, when their initial enthusiasm has vanished, disillusion sets in, and the goal appears more remote than the chances of Switzerland joining the EU.

In a 1984 paper, psychologist Karl Weick asked what you should do when a task (or life itself) looms up like a huge mountain range. Should you tell yourself that you'll conquer it, no matter what? Definitely not.

Any mountaineer will tell you never to look up at the summit when you set out on a climb. If you do, you'll lose heart. Instead, look down at your feet and take one step at a time. At some point, you'll look back and be surprised by how far you have come, just by taking lots of small steps.

When we tackle a new challenge, we quickly start feeling underqualified and overtaxed. It's completely normal, and happens to everyone. But whenever you're tempted to think, "I can't do it!," remind yourself that you're in fact already doing it. One step at a time. Each of us is capable of taking small steps. And every step takes you a tiny, tiny bit closer to your goal. Every step is a little victory.

Weick called the concept "small wins." He argued that "once a small win has been accomplished, forces are set in motion that favor another small win," and that a series of small wins

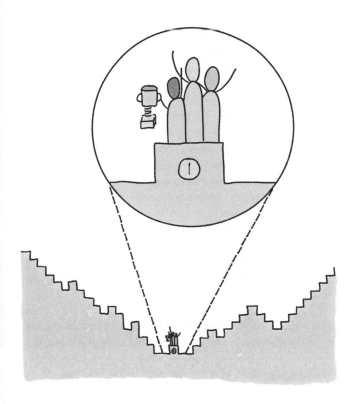

Celebrate the small wins to get you through the lows.

can slowly lead to change – by revealing a pattern which shows us that bigger wins are possible too.

Small failures have a similar, though opposite, effect. When minor losses and discouraging setbacks start piling up, you become so sensitized to disappointment that you start expecting it, and are less inclined to make an effort. All you're thinking is, "This won't work. I'll never be able to do it. Someone else would be better at it."

Of course, Weick wasn't the first person to observe the importance of small wins. As far back as 1903, Rosa Luxemburg formulated a similar strategy, called "revolutionary realpolitik." "Realpolitik," in that you approach your goal with small, achievable steps rather than overthrowing everything all at once; "revolutionary," because this approach "goes, in all the parts of its endeavors, beyond the bounds of the existing order in which it operates." The strategy of small wins, therefore, is not a matter of being content with minor victories and losing sight of your goal – rather, it means not allowing yourself to be discouraged and exhausted by the sheer size of what you're tackling.

This sounds contradictory to what we've been told all this time: most consultants say we should think big, keep our eyes on the benchmark, believe in the vision. But the road is long, and we might stumble, get tired or lose our way. Small losses like that can be as demotivating as small wins can be encouraging.

Now, to return to collaboration: when a team is behind at halftime, when a project runs out of steam and a Tuesday feels like a Friday, start thinking about the small stuff. Celebrate every battle you've won, every completed pass. Small steps take us further too, and even the deepest valley has a podium ready and waiting for you.

TOOLS OF COOPERATION: HOW TO MOTIVATE YOUR TEAM

Say you're planning to climb a mountain with your kids (or grandchildren). Not a *mountain* mountain – you won't need crampons – but still something that requires a fair bit of effort. What is the deciding factor that'll make your little expedition a success?

Clayton Christensen, one of the most influential management theorists of the twentieth century, believed that our culture, i.e. the way we deal with each other, in part decides how far we get. Every company, every group of people, every family has its own culture. "Tools of cooperation" was Christensen's model for how to develop one. There are two key aspects to it. To what extent is everyone in agreement about the goal? And to what extent does everyone agree about the best way to achieve it?

In the context of your hiking expedition, there are four possible outcomes:
1. If people agree neither about whether they want to climb the mountain, nor about how to best get to the top, then the team leader – i.e. you – has to do something to secure everyone's cooperation. You're the boss, so you have to assert yourself. It might sound cold, but if you want to kick-start a culture there's nothing else for it.
2. If you want to do something, but the kids aren't in the mood for a hike (maybe they've never done it before, or

maybe last time was too exhausting), offer them a carrot. "If we get to the top, you can watch YouTube later."

3. If the kids are all keen to climb the mountain but some of them get tired along the way, you have to start leading. People orientate themselves on others, in good things as well as bad. The main driver of toxicity in any company is a toxic boss. Conversely, the more inspiring the leader, the more willing people are to walk through fire – or climb a mountain.

4. If you all want to climb the mountain, and if you all manage to get to the top, it will create a culture where everyone feels motivated. This culture has to be cultivated, though, so when you get back, ask: "Should we do it again next year?" or "What should we do next?"

To reach an extraordinary goal, you sometimes need to resort to extraordinary measures.

SERVANT LEADERSHIP: WHAT DO YOU EXPECT FROM YOUR BOSS?

The question of what makes a good boss is as old as mankind. Presumably every known culture past or present has its conception of leadership. Even in seemingly anarchic situations, there's usually someone in charge. But who, and how?

One interesting leadership style that has come up relatively recently is called "servant leadership," i.e. leading by following. It sounds paradoxical, but isn't really. It means that, instead of leading from the front, you show other people the way and then follow them.

Servant leadership was first defined by Robert Greenleaf in 1970, in an essay in which he distinguished between two different management styles: one that is self-serving, and one that serves others. We're all familiar with the "leader first" style, where what matters is your bonus, your career, your happiness. The "servant first" style turns the pyramid upside down and prioritizes the needs of the team. Leading doesn't mean being the first to conquer the mountain, but making sure that you all get to the top.

This idea is an ancient one. As far as we know, its first appearance in cultural history came in the *Tao Te Ching*. Written by Laozi about 2,500 years ago, it is a sort of anti-Machiavellian instruction manual for anyone who wants to achieve something without hurting other people (or themselves). In chapter 66, Laozi writes:

All rivers flow to the sea,
Because the sea is lower than they.
Its humility gives the sea their power.
If you want to rule people,
You must address them humbly.
If you want to lead people,
You must learn to follow them.

He is speaking here of the power of humility. He uses a powerful metaphor (the oceans collect the waters of the world, because they cover its lowest reaches) and applies it to leadership. By placing themselves in a secondary position – that is, by not putting themselves at the center – leaders are able to collect and unite the water (i.e. the power) of the world's countless streams (i.e. their colleagues).

Leading means serving, not dictating. Leading means enabling others, not proving how good you are. Leading means surrounding yourself with people who are better than you.

LEADER

Servant leadership doesn't mean not leading. It means delegating responsibility to the most competent people in the team.

SERVANT LEADER

REORG: HOW TO CREATE CHANGE

Company restructures, or "reorgs," are rarely a cause for cele-bration for staff. They usually go hand in hand with an announcement that the next few months will be spent getting on top of new processes, or learning something new that will likely be reversed again three months later. Worse, it may mean that your job is at risk.

People are right to worry about these things.

Yet the problem is not that the restructure is a bad idea (though it sometimes is), but that management have under-estimated something seemingly trivial: how long it will take.

Most major upheavals start at the top. One day, the CEO has an urge to change something; or the board have read some-thing about digitalization and AI, and don't want to miss the boat. The CEO pursues the matter, and gets senior manage-ment involved. Together, they come up with different scenarios, and bring in consultants. Months pass. They become more and more convinced that this is the right thing to do, and make a decision. And then, suddenly, everything happens very fast, and management plan to implement their new strat-egy across the company within a matter of weeks.

Company staff hate announcements like that. Not because, as C-level people (i.e. CEOs, CFOs, COOs, etc.) think, they're scared or reluctant to embrace change. It's because they don't have as much time to get used to the idea as management have had.

Management have been toying with the idea for an entire quarter, maybe even longer. Yet the rest of the staff are informed via a single email that the reorg will start in three weeks. It's a bit like harboring doubts about your relationship for years without letting on, and then just leaving your partner one day. Similarly, someone who's only just moved cities can't say on day one whether it was a good idea – they need to settle in first, find out what life in the new place is all about.

Back to reorgs: the best way to handle a big change is to give staff the same amount of time to get used to it – to work out their place in the new order and discover that it might actually be a Good Thing – as management had to come up with it in the first place. Only then start implementing it. The process may take twice as long, but it will be half as painful.

HOW MUCH NEEDS TO CHANGE

The bigger the change, the more time you should give your team.

THE PREMORTEM: HOW
TO AVOID MISTAKES

Gary Klein, a legendary expert in organization development, is a member of the "avoid mistakes" brigade. In the late 1990s, he developed the "premortem method of risk assessment," which doesn't take long at all:

1. Before your project starts, gather your collaborators and pretend to look into a crystal ball. The ball tells you that – damn! – the plan you've been discussing turns out to have been no good. Ask each person to write down the reasons it failed. N.B. don't ask: "What *could* go wrong?" After all, you've already looked into your crystal ball. Instead, ask: "What *went* wrong?"

2. Next, ask everyone to say what, in their opinion, was the main reason the project failed. Write it all down, and then give everyone a chance to evaluate and comment. For example, you could ask everyone to assign a value to the reasons based on how likely or unlikely it is to become an issue.

Sure, your project may fail anyway, but you have now been sensitized to all sorts of mistakes and will be able to avoid them. You will still make mistakes, but different ones. And there's a way to deal with those too (just see the next chapter).

"Before you exchange rings, tell me: what do you
think will cause your marriage to fail?"

THE POSTMORTEM: HOW TO MAKE MISTAKES FASTER

Spotify co-founder Daniel Ek once said: "We aim to make mistakes faster than anyone else."

Sounds a bit silly, doesn't it. The musicians among you would reply: "Yep, you certainly did that." But what exactly did Ek mean?

He probably meant this: if you try something new, you'll make mistakes. And when you're in a competitive environment, it's wise to fail quickly, so that you can quickly learn from your mistakes and quickly improve.

Children are allowed to make mistakes, but adults are not. In fact, adults try to avoid them. Yet if you don't make mistakes, you may never fail, but you won't learn anything either. It's an age-old thought, but a useful one.

Postmortem analysis is an easy and effective way to learn from your mistakes. When a project is done, ask: "What happened? Why did it happen? What are our takeaways? What will we do differently next time?"

The key thing is not to ask: "Who's to blame?" No one will be judged for having done something wrong. Quite the opposite: you're grateful to whoever made a mistake, because they have given you all an opportunity to learn something.

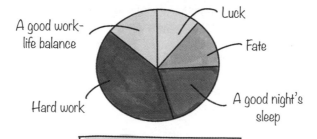

What people say makes someone successful

Luck

Fate

A good night's sleep

Hard work

A good work-life balance

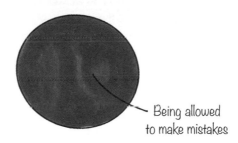

What actually makes us successful

Being allowed to make mistakes

WORKSHOPS: HOW TO HAVE A CONSTRUCTIVE WORKSHOP

If you want to know whether or not you should have a workshop, you need to organize a workshop.

That sentence embodies the whole dilemma of workshops, which, along with meetings, constitute the basic toolkit of any company or organization. Seminar room, coffee, bottled water, flipchart: workshops are the Swiss Army knife of office life. But are they useful?

The short answer is, very – but not always. In our experience, the following helps when thinking about workshops.

A workshop is better than no workshop
If you constantly work in the same old constellation using the same old methods, you'll keep having the same old ideas. Workshop overdose is a well-known phenomenon. The reason they're so exhausting is that they might constitute two hours of fun, but afterward you're still not clear about what you're meant to be doing next. "So, now what?" is a common question among workshop survivors. But they are still a good idea. In fact, every workshop works, no matter what the team – if, that is, you prepare well, have lots of different tasks in your arsenal, ask meaningful questions, increase the intensity toward the end, and include a wrap-up exercise.

Workshops don't suit everyone

One problem with workshops is that there are always some participants whose voice is never heard. They are usually the
introverts in the team, or members who don't enjoy a high status
within the group, or people who aren't sure that their ideas are
any good. Conversely, workshops are dominated by the outgoing,
the self-assured and the loud. One possible solution is to make
sure you include both tasks that require participants to work on
their own and in silence, and group activities with a presentation
element, which will allow extroverts to shine.

Diverse teams will have more surprising ideas

If a boss and an intern unexpectedly find themselves having to
do a presentation together, the hierarchy is dismantled and
conventional thought patterns are disrupted. There is a legendary anecdote about a workshop held by a toothpaste
manufacturer that wanted to increase its turnover. As the team
worked late into the night trying to come up with something, an
office cleaner, who'd been listening to their discussions, sug-
gested they make the hole in the tube bigger. "That's the
problem with cleaning materials – you always end up pouring
out more than you need." Note, however, that not every workshop has to be diverse. If you need a creative solution for the
routing of pre-fader mix subgroups for a 5.1 surround sound
system, it's probably best to invite experts on the subject.

To prepare or not to prepare?

If you, the workshop organizer, send your ten participants a
thirty-page organizational strategy doc, no one will read it.
And it doesn't matter if they don't: workshops thrive on the
here and now. Fresh, unencumbered and cheerful minds may
not produce perfect results, but they'll sometimes produce
unexpected ones. Watch out, though – ad hoc ideas often
prompt suggestions driven by media trends: when climate

change protests are in fashion, ideas will more often than not center on all things green and loud. We've learnt that it's best to provide participants with one small, concrete task by way of preparation. That way, you'll get the well-known "brain dump" – which favors obvious ideas – out of the way before starting your workshop.

CONSENSUS VERSUS CONSENT: WHY NOT EVERYONE HAS TO AGREE

Consensus is the decision-making principle whereby a decision is made only if all members of a team agree. You discuss something until you've found a solution that pleases everyone. In short: consensus exists when everyone's for it.

Consent is the decision-making principle whereby a proposal is agreed to unless someone comes up with a well-founded objection. The operative term here is "well-founded." It isn't enough for someone to take issue with the idea – they need to show that the proposal might foil the team's aims. In short: consent exists when no one's against it.

Consensus has a good reputation. We intuitively think that decisions based on consensus are better than others. We think that there are not only solutions with which everyone agrees, but also solutions that have everyone in raptures. Of course, you do occasionally get pure-as-the-driven-snow consensus, where everyone claps and weeps tears of joy – but it's rare.

Aiming for consensus, for a decision everyone's happy with, is time-consuming and nerve-wracking: some people keep their opinions to themselves, others you can only wish would, and as you search desperately for a common denominator, the idea itself becomes ever more watered down. You care so much about harmony that you lose all sight of the idea. All too often, the result is a lazy compromise.

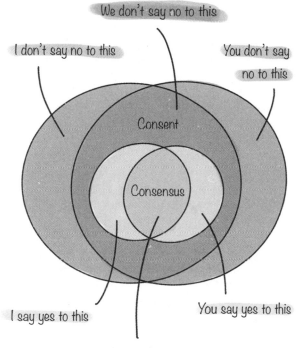

Consent, meanwhile, is consensus's more realistic cousin. When you aim for consent, you're not trying to make everyone happy – rather, your guiding motto is "good enough for now, safe enough to try." It may not be *exactly* what you originally wanted, but if you don't have a better idea, you'll go with it rather than delay the process. Consent doesn't mean that everyone has to agree with the decision. However, once the decision has been made, everyone in the team should back it.

Let's admit it: it's not easy. No one likes backing something they don't like 100 percent. As with so many things, practice makes perfect. A good starting point is for you to announce to the team that, from now on, you'll be making decisions based on consent, not consensus, and explain what that means – i.e. that someone might not always get their way, but that the team will back their proposal another time. (See the next chapter.)

Jeff Bezos has used the phrase "disagree and commit" in connection with consent-based decision-making. In a 2016 letter to shareholders, he wrote: "If you have conviction on a particular direction even though there's no consensus, it's helpful to say, 'Look, I know we disagree on this but will you gamble with me on it?'" He saw it as a way not only to convince others of his ideas, but also to practice putting his trust in others and saying yes to proposals that might not be quite to his taste. You never know, they might actually turn out to be pretty decent.

It's better to help make something happen than to stand in the way of a process. You should welcome the new – otherwise it will go somewhere else.

TWO WORKERS, TWO LEVELS: WHAT'S THE DIFFERENCE BETWEEN FUNCTION AND PURPOSE?

A woman walks past two workers on a building site and asks what they're doing. One replies: "I'm using these bricks to build a wall." The other says: "I'm using these bricks to build a cathedral."

This famous anecdote illustrates how two people can approach the same work from different perspectives. You might say the first worker is focused on the immediate target, while the second is focused on the ultimate goal.

The function of what they are doing is to lay bricks on top of each other, i.e. to create a wall. Their purpose is to build a cathedral.

They both do the same thing, but their points of view differ: the first just wants to "do their job," the second has "a vision."

Both positions are entirely legitimate. It's fine to feel fulfilled by earning a living and having a nine-to-five job. Yet it's no secret that people who see the purpose of what they do are happier at work (see *Purpose*, p. 102).

The question for a team leader is how to handle these two different perspectives. There are three possible approaches:

This is not a brick.*

*It's the start of a cathedral.

1. Try to get everyone to perceive the same reality

Remind your team of the project's goal – and that there is one. Do it more than once, not just when you launch the project. Also, keep elaborating it. What are we building? Why are we building a cathedral? What will it look like? How much – and what – is still missing?

2. Accept that everyone has a different perception of reality

No matter how well and how often you reiterate point 1, people will have different opinions on the purpose of your endeavor. Some will enthusiastically absorb it; others will never be quite sure what it's all about. In such cases, you could try to turn purpose into function: "Let's make the best bricks we can, and deliver them on time." (It will make the team member who's building a cathedral very happy.) Not everyone needs to identify with the purpose, but everyone needs to understand that their function *serves* a purpose.

3. Increase understanding between the two groups

It's not only the builders whose understanding of the purpose of the project might differ. There are other departments too – architects, structural engineers, the construction company, etc. It's crucial for everyone to be informed both about the cathedral and about the bricklaying: you'll often find that the people involved in the project are more interested in the cathedral than you thought, and merely don't have enough time to think about it, or believe that if they do it will distract from their day-to-day work. Conversely, if the "visionaries" want to properly understand the foundations of the cathedral, they need to properly understand the function of bricklaying.

This is sometimes called the "two workers, two levels" theory. Ask your collaborators: what are your bricks? When will your wall be finished? What is your cathedral?

PURPOSE: WHAT'S THE DIFFERENCE BETWEEN A VISION, A MISSION AND A PURPOSE?

There is a fine line between the three, but we find the following definitions by consultant Andreas Diehl particularly useful:

- "Vision" is the answer to the question: "What will our future look like?" It points us in the direction in which we need to go, or in which we need to evolve.
- "Mission" is the answer to the question: "What guides our day-to-day work?" It tells us the concrete things we need to do here and now, so that we can keep advancing toward our vision.
- "Purpose" is the answer to the question: "Why do we do what we do?" It's about the meaning of our work.

It doesn't matter whether you consider your vision, mission and purpose individually or together. What's important is that you think about what you're doing and why, and that you make sure everyone in your organization sees things the same way.

In 2009, visions, missions and purposes got a boost when Simon Sinek came up with the concept of the "golden circle." He argued that most companies define themselves by *what* they do. Only then do they ask themselves *how* they do what they do, and only after that – if at all – are they interested in *why* they are doing it. He proposed that organizations should handle things the other way round: first decide *why* you do what you do, then decide *how* you want to do it – and the first two will then lead you to the *what*. This approach alone won't

guarantee success, but it's well worth checking once in a while whether everyone's clear about what you are doing it all for.

But what do we do with our purpose now? What is *the meaning of* the meaning of what we do? In our experience, the following are some of its key functions (there may be others):

Purpose as the common denominator
Your purpose statement doesn't have to sound good. It isn't a slogan, to be devised by clever copywriters. Rather, it's the common denominator agreed by those involved in a given process, and which you regularly return to and renegotiate. Your position statement will sound superficial only to outsiders, who weren't there when you developed and negotiated it. However, it will be meaningful to anyone who was part of that decision and is implementing it at work every day.

Purpose as a decision-marking tool
"Should we change our opening hours?" "Should we introduce product A or product B?" "Should I change careers?" Questions such as these are best answered by weighing your options in the light of your ultimate purpose. If recalling your purpose doesn't help, it will mean one of two things: either your purpose isn't precise enough, or whatever decision you make won't affect it.

Purpose as a recruitment tool
Teamwork works best when the convictions of the company and the staff coincide, and perhaps even reinforce one another. If your purpose is clear, you should spell it out in the job description: explain what your company stands for, where you're heading and the kind of person you'd like to have with you along the way. At interview stage, ask the candidates

more about their own purpose: that is, don't just ask yourself whether *they* will fit in, but whether *their outlook* will.

Purpose as compass

If an organization doesn't have a clear purpose, departments and staff will decide for themselves what they are or are not working toward. You'll end up with that fearsome silo mentality, where the general goal ends up competing with special interests. A strong purpose, understood and backed by all, can prevent this from happening.

NORTH STAR METRICS: YOU DON'T NEED A TRAVEL GUIDE – YOU NEED A GOAL

The Big Dipper is the most prominent constellation in our night sky. Any child can spot it. Four stars make the frame of the bowl; three stars form the handle. In the old days, this constellation was a key navigational aid: if you extend the invisible line connecting the two stars at the back end of the bowl by five times its length, you'll arrive at the North Star.

For seafarers and other travelers, the North Star is a reliable signpost. In the course of the night, all other stars wander across the sky – Polaris is the only one that remains still. If someone is lost, all they need to do to find their way is look up at the night sky.

Honestly, who doesn't wish they had a fixed point like that to guide them through life? Or at least through their working life?

The North Star Metric (NSM) is used as a reference point for all actions taken by a company or other organization.

The NSM shouldn't be confused with a company's purpose or vision. It determines, rather, whether or not you are still working toward the ultimate goal.

To determine the NSM, you first need to define your goal. It's no good knowing where north is if you don't know where you're going.

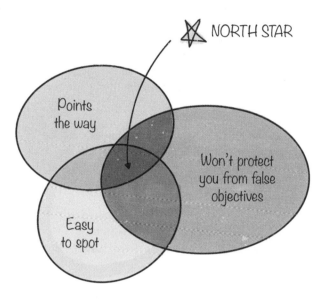

Let's take an example:
Netflix's overarching aim is "to entertain the world." But what does that mean, and how can you measure it?

Divide your goal into measurable units. For Netflix, it is the time people spend watching its output. This is now the star toward which all activity points.

It doesn't mean that Netflix doesn't use other metrics too. Of course, every team and every staff member has their own KPIs (key performance indicators) against which to measure their performance. But they should all feed into the "North Star goal."

You can even take the North Star as a concrete guide. If you lose your way among all the day-to-day stress, briefly ask yourself before you send an email, invest money or give a presentation: "Will it help make audiences spend longer watching?" If yes, do it. If no, don't.

These days, lots of companies work with NSM. It is a technique that aligns more closely to Silicon Valley's philosophy than any other framework:

- The whole team commits to the same goal.
- A ruthless yes/no matrix decides whether or not the goal is being reached. Netflix has either gained more viewing minutes, or it hasn't. There is no room for ambiguity, interpretation or conversations about matters of taste.

This Silicon Valley–style total focus on numbers can be damaging too. By appointing a specific metric as your Polaris, you are at the same time defining what is important – that is, what is a priority and what isn't. What you measure, grows.

So be careful what you measure.

The North Star is an orientation, not a travel guide. It is a signpost, not a finish line. You yourself have to work out what your goal is, identify the dangers that lurk along the way and decide whether you maybe want to go somewhere else instead.

SAYING YES: WHY EVERY TEAM NEEDS A YES-PERSON

This book was written by two people. Mikael usually says yes. Roman usually says no. Who's right?

Mikael believes that saying yes makes you happy.

When you say yes, you open yourself up to new possibilities. You become more accepting and more willing to try new things, and you have more experiences.

Saying yes usually triggers positive feelings in your interlocutor too. Who doesn't like having their request, invitation or suggestion answered with a yes? And the happiness prompted by your yes reflects back on you, and makes you a little happier too.

Contact with other people begins with a yes. Yes, I'll come to the family event (even though I'm really busy). Yes, I'll help clean up the community garden (even though I'd rather be watching Netflix). Yes, I'll meet you for a coffee (even though I'm not in a great mood).

Of course, not every yes is a good yes. It's never a good idea to say yes in a situation when you'd rather say no. However, we remember the good more than the bad – we feel nostalgia not because the old days were better, but because we've forgotten the bad stuff.

SAYING NO: WHY EVERY TEAM NEEDS A NAYSAYER

This book was written by two people. Mikael usually says yes. Roman usually says no. Who's right?

Roman believes that saying no makes you happy.

Initially, it's hard to say no to someone. Will they be disappointed? Will we miss out on a once-in-a-lifetime opportunity? Yet people know that you can't say yes to everything, and an unequivocal "I'm afraid I can't" is less unpleasant than a tentative "I'll try to make it."

Requests or invitations are often issued far in advance. You tell yourself that, although you are stressed *now*, when the time comes you'll no doubt find room in your schedule. But if you're honest with yourself, you know that, as the date approaches, you'll wish you hadn't said yes. If, instead, you say no right away, you're signaling to the other person that you put your all into your projects, so you like to focus on just a few. It might make you unpopular at first, because the other person is disappointed that you said no, but in the long run it will garner you more respect, because you are realistic about your time and energy resources.

Saying no is always also a yes. When you decline new requests and contacts, you are acknowledging the requests and contacts you once said yes to. A no signals loyalty, not a lack of interest.

<u>WHAT I MEAN WHEN I SAY NO</u>

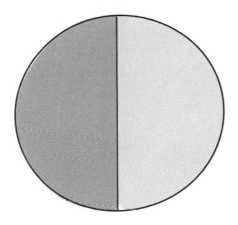

■ I'd like to, but I don't have time

□ Sounds tempting – but I know if I say yes
I'll immediately regret it

■ I don't like you

Creating Trust

CORPORATE CULTURE: WILL WE GET FREE APPLES?

Do you have a fresh fruit basket in your office? Does your boss offer mindfulness training, hybrid readiness workshops, stress management courses, foosball and a nap room?

Good. In that case, your company understands that it has to improve the way it deals with its toxic corporate culture.

On the one hand.

On the other hand, it might be better if the company improved its corporate culture, rather than the way it deals with it.

A lot of research has been done on this, and the findings always essentially center on the following:

How about not teaching people how to deal with insecurity, but making them feel more secure? What if we didn't train people how to be resilient, but fired abusive bosses? What if we got rid of oppressive rules and stopped micromanaging staff, rather than spending time refining our position statement? What if, instead of installing a slide in the office, we paid people more and offered them better contract terms? Why always try to increase efficiency, rather than simply give staff more time and fewer tasks to do?

Mindfulness, positive thinking and team-building activities are powerful techniques. They can be incredibly helpful, and we keep writing about them in a positive light here too. However, the problem is that they allow organizations to get away with ever more precarious employment terms and tougher cuts, by transferring responsibility to their staff: you have to change your life; you have to work on yourself; if you're stressed, that's your fault, not ours.

Many organizations try to find individual solutions to structural problems.This is a problem.

Do set up the foosball table and get out the yoga mats – but only *after* you've secured the safety, trust and respect of your staff. And then buy one or more rounds of drinks.

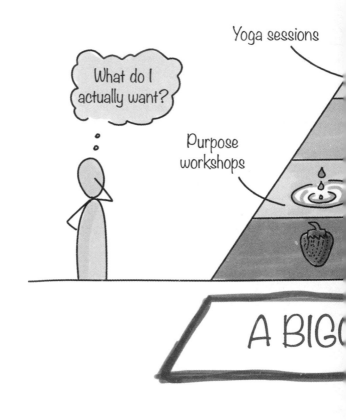

Maslow's hierarchy of needs.

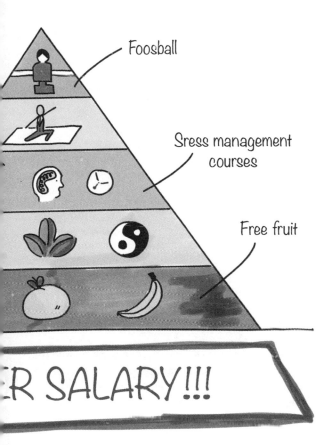

Foosball

Sress management
courses

Free fruit

R SALARY!!!

TEAM CULTURE: WHAT MAKES A TEAM BOND

What would you say are the most important qualities you'd like to see in your colleagues and collaborators – aside from being skilled at what they do? Team spirit? Loyalty? Ambition? Friendliness?

When basketball coach Steve Kerr decided to speak to his team on this subject, he listed the following: joy, mindfulness, compassion and competition.

Kerr is not just any old basketball coach: his Golden State Warriors are considered the best team of the past decade. When Kerr started coaching them, they were merely average. (You suspect that we're about to embark on a tale of athletic success, filled with pathos – but bear with us.)

The secret of Kerr's success is not that he came up with the four core values of joy, mindfulness, compassion and competition. Such terms are frequently mentioned in kick-off workshops – and then never again. No, what was special about his statement was that these core values weren't merely scribbled on a flipchart. They actually became the Warriors' mantra.

Francesca Gino and Jeff Huizinga from Harvard Business School even published an excellent article about Kerr's fascinating leadership principle.

The idea of introducing a team mantra came to Kerr when he spent two weeks shadowing the Seattle Seahawks coach, Pete Carroll, in preparation for his new role as the Warriors' head coach. One day, Carroll asked him: "How are you going to coach your team?" "You mean, like, what offense are we going to run?" "No, that stuff doesn't matter," said Carroll. "I'm talking about what your day is going to look like. What practice will feel like. What are the players going to feel when they walk into your building?"

Kerr thought long and hard about it. On Carroll's advice, he wrote down the ten things that were most important to him in life: authenticity, teamwork, empathy, vulnerability, humor, etc. A few long talks with Carroll later, Kerr condensed these to the four values that had guided his life in the past, and which he wanted his players to have: joy, mindfulness, compassion and competition.

The mantra of a team – or of a company – is not the same as its vision. Rather, the mantra represents the culture that feeds into the vision. It reflects your mindset, your attitude toward what you do and the way you work. Every business has its own particular culture; the question is whether it forms by accident, or whether you actively choose and cultivate it.

This is how Kerr explained his mantra, i.e. the culture he wanted to foster in the team, to the players:

Joy
Good things happen when you do things you enjoy. Show me that you're having fun.

Mindfulness

Be conscious that you are spending every day doing what you love most – playing basketball. Knowing this will make you feel grateful, and help you overcome injury, crises and losses.

Compassion

We can only win together. If another player makes a mistake, don't roll your eyes. Instead, go up to him and high-five him. You might measure our success by whether we win the championship – I measure it based on how well you treat each other.

Competition

What is the best possible version of you? And how can I help you to become it?

Who wouldn't like their team to be a little bit like the Golden State Warriors?

THE TRUST TRIANGLE: HOW TO BUILD TRUST

When we talk about trust, what we usually mean is things like: "Can I trust this person?" We rarely think of things like: "Can this person trust me?"

The phrase "trust-building measures" is a bit of a mouthful, but it may just be the most important phrase for any leader. Trust is key to collaboration. Once you stop constantly evaluating and controlling others, once you stop worrying about whether they'll stick with you, whether they can do the job or whether they'll show up for work tomorrow, you will feel calmer and more confident.

If you're a leader and want to build trust within your team, you first have to change the way you look at things. Shift your focus from results to the people who are supposed to achieve those results. It sounds like a small change, but it makes a huge difference. So take a moment and ask yourself what you are currently focusing on.

Frances Frei and Anne Morriss introduced the "trust triangle" in their excellent book *Unleashed: The Unapologetic Leader's Guide to Empowering Everyone Around You*. They argue that trust is driven by three key factors: authenticity, empathy and logic. People trust you because you are honest, open and don't have a secret agenda (authenticity), because they feel you care about them (empathy) and because your decisions are reasonable and your actions are plausible (logic)

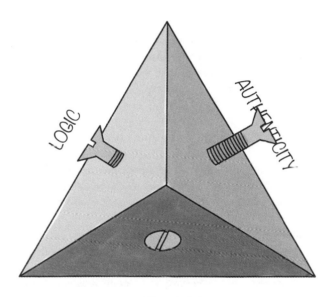

EMPATHY

Which of your screws is loose?

When a team no longer trust each other, you will usually discover some kind of disturbance in one of those three factors. To rebuild trust, you have to find out which of them has started "wobbling," which screw has come loose. When it comes to trust, we all have our weaknesses; we are all wobbly somewhere. To discover which is the errant screw, Frei and Morriss suggest trying this: think of a time when someone trusted you less than you'd have liked. Are you picturing it? Now do this – and it won't be easy: tell yourself that the other person was right. Assume that their reservations were well founded, and that their lack of trust in you was your fault.

Authenticity
Ask yourself: *Did I truly believe what I said back then?*

If the answer is no, you have an authenticity problem. It's fine to play different roles in different situations – but Frei and Morriss argue that, in the long run, it pays to be frank.

Empathy
Ask yourself: *Did I put my own interests above the team's?*

If the answer is yes, you have an empathy problem. Frei and Morriss argue that people who are analytical and hungry for knowledge often have a problem with compassion. They become impatient with people who aren't motivated by the same things or who take longer to get to grips with something. And their collaborators can sense it.

Logic
Ask yourself: *Did my plans sound reasonable and convincing?*

If not, you have a logic problem. In this case, Frei and Morriss suggest that you review the data, and only talk about the things you know to be true. Then practice communicating your ideas effectively: your logic may only *seem* wobbly because you are not communicating it well enough. People need to trust in your ability to execute your plans, so make their basis clear and compelling and show that you have a strong grasp of the facts.

This exercise works best when your sparring partner is someone who knows you and can assess you correctly. Now comes the hardest part: check whether your evaluation of the event in question is correct by talking openly about it to the person who didn't trust you back then.

Frei and Morriss believe that we can start rebuilding trust only by having that conversation.

SUTTON'S GOOD AND BAD BOSSES: WHAT YOURS IS PROBABLY DOING WRONG

Several years ago, in his book *Good Boss, Bad Boss*, Bob Sutton – professor at the Stanford Graduate School of Business and a true guiding light in organizational and occupational psychology – observed that you can recognize a good leader from the fact that they understand what it feels like to work for them.

His book is obviously about many other things too, but let's focus on this point: Sutton argues that it is key for leaders to be aware of the effect they have on others. It might sound trivial, but a whole gamut of studies in social psychology have shown that the more power we have, the more we put ourselves at the center and the less we're interested in other people.

So if you want to be a good boss, you should urgently ask yourself: how does it feel to work for me?

Now, it isn't easy to know what effect you have on other people. One radical way to do it is to ask a neutral third party to interview your staff (anonymously, of course). But Sutton says that you can also discover the answer by asking three questions:

1. How much do I talk compared with others?
This is about finding out whether you're focused more on yourself or on others. You can do so relatively easily by asking

GOOD BOSS:

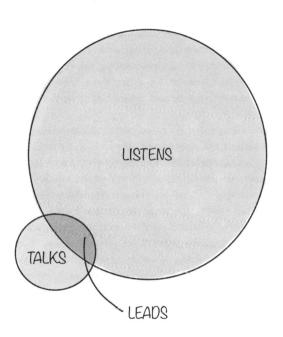

What's your ratio?

someone you trust to come to one of your meetings and note down how long you talk for, compared with how long the others talk for. Compare the two. (It's also interesting to see how much time women and men spend talking in the meeting.)

2. How often do I ignore, interrupt or cut other people short?

It's totally fine to interrupt others occasionally in a meeting, e.g. when they're talking nonsense or when you've just had a great idea. It's what makes discussions lively. But if you do it constantly, it suggests that you don't listen and don't try to understand the thoughts and feelings of others.

3. When I do speak, how often do I make statements, and how often do I ask questions?

Sutton says that bad bosses often have strong views on anything and everything. This is in part because everyone expects leaders to have an opinion. However, leaders also tend to think they're the smartest person in the room. This isn't a problem in itself – who knows, maybe they are. But there's something else at the heart of it: we believe that when we talk, we are leading. However, the truth is that we lead when we enable others to exceed themselves. The more we talk, the less we listen, and the less we understand the other person's frame of mind, what bothers them, what they are thinking; and the less we give them a chance to improve. In short: the more you talk, the less you're leading.

Our conception of bosses is sheer cliché: a good boss, we think, is charismatic and exudes self-confidence. But if you read Sutton's book, you'll realize that the opposite of "self-confident" isn't "unconfident" but "modest." It isn't about being good, it's about making others better.

In short, it's not you who has to be charismatic. Your job is to give others an opportunity to be charismatic.

BUILDING A TEAM: WHY "VULNERABLE" IS THE NEW "STRONG"

When people come together to do something, they have to be able to count on each other. There has to be trust. Yet trust doesn't happen of its own accord – you have to *build* it. You have to *build* your team. The surest way to build trust is to experience an adventure together.

The reason for this is that when we find ourselves in an extreme situation, at some point we stop pretending that we are strong and calm and know what's what. At some point, we take off our armor and show our "true" self. We reveal our vulnerability. Moments like that are quite extreme, and no one likes showing their weakness. But when we do, something amazing happens: trust happens.

This process is sometimes called the "vulnerability loop." In his book *The Culture Code*, Daniel Coyle describes it as follows:

Person A shows their vulnerability.
Person B realizes, and shows their own vulnerability.
Now Person A feels less bad about it.
They agree it's OK to be vulnerable.

The decisive factor in this scenario is Person B's reaction. When someone admits to a weakness, and you act as if you don't have any weaknesses yourself, that person will never again admit to one. No one else in the room will either. That way, a culture of toughness is born. However, if you too admit to a weakness, others will feel emboldened to do the same, which creates a culture of vulnerability.

Why is it good for people to be vulnerable? Simple: because it means that, when you're in a group setting, you'll be happy to say things like: "I'm not sure I can do this alone. Can you help?," "I have a crazy idea," "I'm sorry I said that," "I was wrong."

Vulnerability is not a weakness. It encourages honesty and openness, inspires, and fosters creativity.

Building trust is a slow process. This is especially true when a team has previously been negatively affected by difficult colleagues or toxic leadership. Survival training won't fix this, so you must practice respect, kindness and courtesy every day. The vulnerability loop is a good launchpad. To create a culture of vulnerability, and therefore trust, start with a round of questions like: "What's your name, and why?," or "What was your favorite book as a kid?," or "When did you last do something for the first time?" Asking essentially harmless questions such as these at the start of your project, workshop or meeting will help create a congenial atmosphere.

THE XY THEORY: WHAT KIND OF EMPLOYEE ARE YOU?

People who say that everyone is different aren't wrong, but you could also see things Douglas McGregor's way. In *The Human Side of Enterprise* (1960), he distinguished between two fundamental employee types: X and Y. X-types work to earn money. They don't like discussions, they want announcements. To motivate them, their manager needs to hand out tasks and incentives. Y-types work better when they feel they have a say. To motivate them, the manager needs to foster a sense of commitment.

In 1981, William Ouchi revealed that many of us see ourselves as Y-types, but still prefer the path of an X-type. There is, he argued, a third, blended type: Z. Z-types want security, which they repay with loyalty. For a manager, it means offering long-term (Ouchi even suggests lifelong) employment contracts. Z-people talk about autonomy, but what they need is support. This means that they need to be coached. Z-people also rate interaction and atmosphere more highly than success, so the happier the employee, the better they will perform.

Ouchi's Z-type management style is reminiscent of good parenting: it's a question of finely balancing freedom and control.

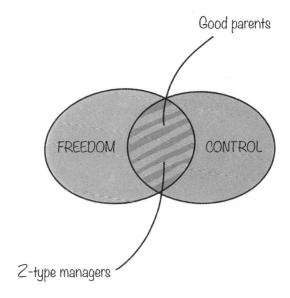

We all need rules, even if only so we can break them.

DIVERSITY: WHY YOU SHOULD EMPLOY PEOPLE WHO ARE NOT LIKE YOU

We instinctively trust people who are similar to us. If someone speaks with the same accent, listens to the same music or went to the same school as us, we automatically feel closer to them, without even knowing it. Shared backgrounds, experiences and tastes give us a sense of security – which is why we usually like working with people we'd also want to have a drink with.

That's why, when we put together a team, we unconsciously tend to choose people who are like us. This is called "hiring for culture fit." Hiring for culture fit is nice, because it means that everyone thinks alike. But it isn't useful, because it means that everyone thinks alike.

Instead, you should hire people who extend, rather than mirror you. This is called "hiring for culture contribution." Diversity trumps uniformity.

Hearing the word "diversity" usually makes us think of ethnicity or gender. But diversity is about more than that. People from certain classes or other cultural backgrounds, people with disabilities or mental health issues, and people who are deemed "too young" or "too old," often find it hard to secure employment or promotion.

When putting a team together, you should therefore think carefully about the qualities, talents, strengths and skills that you need and that would augment your organization or team – and especially also about the voices you are missing.

Diversity of thought, experience and background is beneficial for any team. However, a diverse team alone is not automatically a recipe for success. At first, it may lack the common knowledge base that is crucial to making sure that both team and project thrive. But if you create the sorts of conditions that enable everyone to contribute their individual perspectives and experiences, you will actually expand the cumulative knowledge base on which the team can draw. In an inclusive environment, a diverse team will outperform a homogeneous one – studies have shown that in all sorts of contexts, diverse teams consistently and unequivocally have the edge.

With this in mind, it's worth remembering that the work isn't over at recruitment stage. If you want an *inclusive* team, not just a diverse one, you need to invest time, and be open and flexible. Your purpose statement will be more important than ever, as will your framing of targets and ultimate goals, and your role distribution, organization structure and leadership styles.

The result? Better outcomes for everyone.

THE MORE DIVERSE...

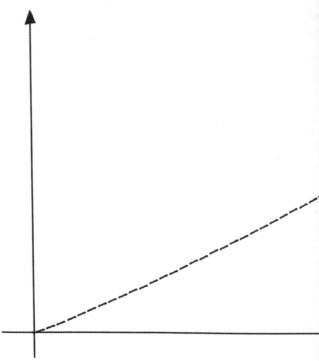

#dreamteam

...THE
BETTER*

*and the more effort it may require

PERFORMANCE VERSUS TRUST: HOW TO SELECT THE RIGHT CANDIDATES

The general consensus is that people are the single most important factor when it comes to a business's success or failure. But how do you know whether someone is right for your team?

Simon Sinek has provided one of the simplest, yet surprising, answers to this question. (Anyone who has ever spent time on LinkedIn will be familiar with his two-minute video clip on the subject. It's worth watching it more than once.) The Navy Seals once told Sinek that whenever they choose a new member they use a performance versus trust matrix (see illustration). The "performance" axis determines the extent to which a candidate meets their requirements; the "trust" axis determines what kind of person they are. In the Navy Seals' macho parlance: "I may trust you with my life" (performance), "but do I trust you with my money and my wife?" (trust).

The candidates are subsequently categorized as one of four types:

Low performer, low trust: someone no one wants

High performer, high trust: someone everyone wants

High performer, low trust: someone who seems good, but isn't

Low performer, high trust: someone who doesn't seem good, but is.

The interesting fact to note here is that the Navy Seals rate

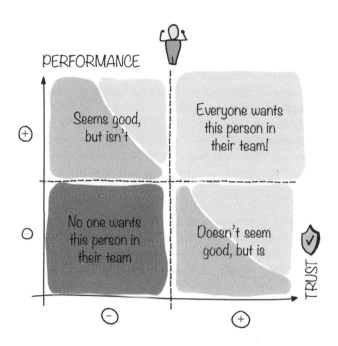

trust higher than performance. They would rather employ a low performer they trust than a high performer they don't trust. They aren't looking for someone who's good at everything, but someone everyone in the team can rely on. As Sinek explains, what they're after is someone who, even in extreme mental or physical situations, finds the strength to help their fellow operatives.

Of course, the Navy Seals are an outlier. Most teams don't need elite soldiers – but they also don't need someone who manages to break the photocopier while making coffee. Have a think about Sinek's anecdote, and ask yourself: "What do I value more when it comes to my colleagues: high performance, or the feeling that I can trust them? What kind of people have I worked with better up to now, in the course of my career?"

We suspect your answer to this last question will be: "With people whom I trusted." This means two things: someone you can rely on to perform, but also someone you can rely on as a person. It's obvious, really; but in annual reviews and when setting objectives, the conversation almost exclusively centers on performance – hardly ever on trust. The vast majority of companies measure their management teams based on performance (sales, quarterly results, etc.), but practically ignore the question of how much they trust them.

LIFT-OUT: WHY YOU SHOULD
CHANGE JOBS AS A TEAM

A little warm-up question. Would you prefer to fly with a crew who are:

a. well rested, but don't know each other very well yet, or
b. tired, but have worked with each other many times before?

Hopefully, you choose (b). Better fly with a crew who haven't slept enough the night before, but who know each other well. Seventy-three percent of all air accidents happen when it's the crew's first time flying together. NASA once conducted a simulation, and unequivocally found that a well-rested team flying together for the first time makes more mistakes than a tired team, who might have just done a twelve-hour shift but have flown together lots of times before.

You'll find similar statistics in medicine too. Heart-bypass operation fatality rates are lowest in hospitals with a well-established team of cardiac surgeons, anesthesiologists and surgical nurses.

We can say, then, that a team's performance doesn't depend on the performance of individual members, but first and foremost on how well they work together, and on the context. The high-flyer who excels in company A won't necessarily do so in company B. Every star needs a team.

What exactly does this mean for you?

For employees

Don't just look for a job that interests you, but for a company and an environment that suit you. Don't merely ask yourself: "What will I be doing?" but always also: "Who will be my colleagues?" Once you've found a group of colleagues you work well with, try to stay together as a team.

For employers

Don't look for individuals – look for teams. Even the most gifted person needs an environment in which they can shine. When you hire a talented candidate, try to hire the team that has made the candidate as good as they are at the same time. In HR, the process of hiring entire teams is called "lift-out." Sure, it's cheaper to recruit just one person, but cheap is expensive in the long run: what if the candidate was only able to shine in their previous job thanks to the team around them? But don't just *hire* whole teams. Go further. Reward whole teams. Promote whole teams.

What I can do

It's our fellow team members who help us grow, not the things we do.

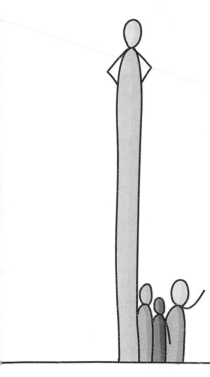

What I can do when I have
Julia, Azra and Tom
by my side

FLAT HIERARCHIES: HOW TO CREATE SPACE FOR SOMETHING NEW

Frederick the Great, ruler of Prussia from 1740 to 1786, was fascinated by mechanical toys that all looked the same and moved the same, and wanted to turn his soldiers into similarly standardized beings. Alongside making sure the troops all received identical training, the key element in his plan was the chain of command, where a superior rank issues orders that are carried out by the subordinate ranks – hierarchy writ large.

A hierarchy's chief strength is that everything goes according to plan. The process and the result are predictable, and this creates stability.

A hierarchy's chief weakness is, ironically, that everything goes according to plan. There is no room for the new. In addition, the decision-making process is long-winded and cumbersome, which stifles change.

Frederick the Great suspected this too, so he added decentralized units which were allowed to act autonomously. Thus hierarchy's most enthusiastic champion also became the father of the flat hierarchy. When someone says "flat hierarchy," many people think of a world where everyone has a say and no one has the last word. Not at all. Rather, "flat" means a structure with as few rungs on the ladder as possible – and typically without middle management. It shortens the lines of communication from plan to execution, making the process faster and more direct. It gives staff more room to maneuver, more flexibility and independence, and they will take more responsibility for what they do. Crucially, however, overall responsibility remains with the leadership: if your staff don't have recourse to someone in charge, they will find their newly acquired elbow room onerous rather than liberating.

A flat hierarchy, then, means giving staff an opportunity to shape the business, while senior management retains responsibility for the overall end result. It sounds like a good idea, doesn't it? You'll no doubt find few people who'd prefer a role in the ranks of the Prussian army to a flat hierarchy.

Yet in practice, a flat hierarchy often doesn't translate into departments that are free from restrictive guidelines. It frequently means that they are set certain targets (usually financial ones) while being provided with only limited means and opportunities to achieve them, or even none at all. Responsibility is thereby shifted downward, while leaving staff without a mandate to truly change anything.

"If we spread it out on the floo

ur hierarchy will look flat too."

SOCIOCRACY: WHAT #NEWWORK MIGHT LOOK LIKE

For a long time, people thought that a pyramid was the best structure for organizing people and work. They weren't entirely wrong. Clear hierarchies do guarantee order and stability. But there are increasing signs that this organization model no longer works. Staff are exhausted – and so are their managers.

The reasons for the general exhaustion are manifold. According to Frederic Laloux, author of the groundbreaking *Reinventing Organizations*, one of them is the fact that pyramid structures don't take the complexity of the modern world into account. Many others agree.

There is an alternative: organize people into a circle, instead of a pyramid. This is called a sociocracy – a government of associates.

Simply put, each circle, or team, in the organization looks after one aspect of the work needed to achieve the company's goal, and takes sole responsibility for it. The circle shows where the team's area of autonomy begins and ends, making it clear for which decisions the circle has sole responsibility. Some circles will overlap, and some roles will appear in more than one circle. The core idea is self-management, i.e. giving the teams in each circle as much freedom as possible, while ensuring that the work done by the various circles serves the organization's higher purpose (see *Agility*, p. 30).

For some people, this sounds a bit like sitting round a bonfire singing "Kumbaya." But if you take a closer look at the fundamental principles guiding sociocratic workplaces, you'll immediately think: "I'd love to work somewhere like that."

1. Equality: everyone affected by a decision is involved in the decision.
2. Consent: act only when all objections have been taken into account (see *Consensus versus Consent*, p. 94).
3. Responsibility: keep your word, and act in everyone's best interest.
4. Continuous improvement: divide the path to your goal into small steps, and learn as you go along – so that you can perform the next step even better (see *Small Wins*, p. 70).
5. Transparency: make all information available to everyone in your organization, unless there's an important reason to keep certain things confidential.
6. Effectiveness: only do things that take you closer to your goal.
7. Empiricism: keep testing your assumptions, and adjust them if necessary.

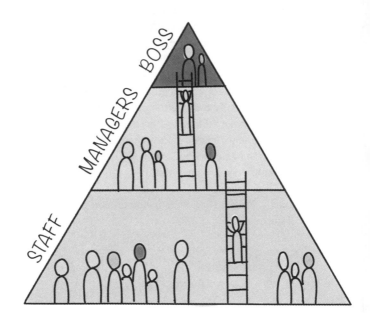

Convert your triangle into circles.

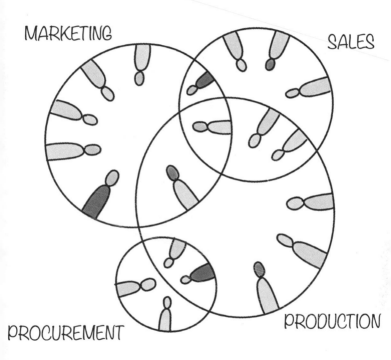

NUNCHI: HOW MUCH ARE YOU CONTRIBUTING TO THE TEAM?

The ancient principle of nunchi is deeply rooted in Korea's Confucian history. It is the art of sensing other people's mood. At its center is the idea of "space." It can be a physical place, such as a conference room; or non-physical – a situation in which you encounter others, e.g. meeting friends at a bar, sitting down to dinner with your family, being called into your boss's office or going into your daughter's bedroom. It's about sensing the other person's frame of mind, "reading the room" and working out what the room "needs" – i.e. how to improve the mood or ease the tension.

Good nunchi means quickly understanding the kind of social space you're in and what you can do to make others feel comfortable. The Korean-American journalist Euny Hong describes it in her fantastic book *Nunchi: The Korean Secret to Happiness and Success* as a particularly Eastern concept. We in the Western world may also pay attention to other people's reactions, but only to the extent that they affect us. We care about whether we are seen, whether our message has come across and what effect we have on others. In Korea, the reverse applies. The idea is that you should "read" others, and focus on what they need and how you might have a positive influence on them.

How good is your nunchi? When you're in a meeting, do you notice when someone has something to say, but is reluctant to express their opinion? Do you check that everyone's

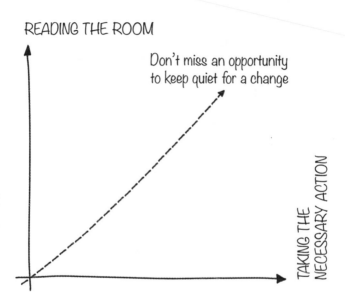

READING THE ROOM

Don't miss an opportunity
to keep quiet for a change

TAKING THE
NECESSARY ACTION

This is particularly valid for men.

already had a piece of chocolate before you take the last one? If yes, you probably have good nunchi. Do people have a tendency to shift in their seats or even roll their eyes when you explain God and the world to them yet again? Are you often asked: "Didn't you notice?" Do you always have to have the last word? Then you probably need to work on your nunchi.

Still, it isn't enough to grasp the situation and work out what's going on. Nunchi means *reading* the situation – and then taking responsibility for it. We can't expect people to change; it's down to us to introduce the change we want. If you notice that a meeting is running out of steam, or that a one-to-one is getting tense, there's no point in merely observing the fact. Do something about it.

At first, nunchi sounds altruistic. Yet there is a decidedly Machiavellian aspect to it. You need nunchi to get along with people, but you also need it to get what you want. The idea is that, instead of taking something you want, you make others willingly give you what you really need.

If you want to practice nunchi, do the following: before you enter a room, take a deep breath and ask yourself what you'll be carrying in with you. Are you tired? Stressed? Hungry? Irritable? And don't confuse the general mood in the room with your own.

When you meet up with someone, remember that it's not all about you. Ask yourself: "What can I do to make sure the other person is comfortable? What can I do to ensure that their voice is heard, to encourage them to have fresh ideas or to say what they really think?" To achieve what you want to achieve, spend less time talking in meetings, and instead listen carefully to what others have to say.

And for God's sake stop insisting on having the last word. In short, nunchi means: when you're in a meeting, never pass on a good opportunity to shut up (Euny Hong).

Appendix

SOURCES

The Two-Pizza Rule
Janet Choi, "Why Jeff Bezos' Two-Pizza Team Rule Still Holds True in 2018," I Done This, 4 December 2018.

Tuckman's Stages
Kate Cassidy, "Tuckman Revisited: Proposing a New Model of Group Development for Practitioners," *Journal of Experiential Education* 29:3, 2007.

Aron Warren, *In-Depth Look at Tuckman's Ladder and Subsequent Works as a Tool for Managing a Project Team*, SANS White Paper, March 2017.

Bruce Tuckman, "Developmental Sequence in Small Groups," *Psychological Bulletin* 63:6, 1965.

Run the Bank versus Change the Bank
Shane Parrish and Rhiannon Beaubien, *The Great Mental Models*, Vol. 1 (Ottawa: Latticework Publishing, 2019).

Hybrid Work
Longqi Yang et al., "The Effects of Remote Work on Collaboration Among Information Workers," *Nature Human Behaviour* 6, 2022.

Mary Baker, "4 Modes of Collaboration Are Key to Success in Hybrid Work," Gartner, 14 June 2021.

New Pay
Gary Charness et al., "The Hidden Advantage of Delegation: Pareto Improvements in a Gift Exchange Game," *American Economic Review* 102:5, 2012.

Wesley C. King, Edward W. Miles and D. David Day, "A Test and Refinement of the Equity Sensitivity Construct," *Journal of Organizational Behavior* 14:4, 1993.

Red Team versus Blue Team
Mark Yanalitis, "Red Teaming Approach, Rationale, and Engagement Risks," ResearchGate, January 2014.

Agility
Henrik Kniberg and Anders Ivarsson, "Scaling Agile @ Spotify with Tribes, Squads, Chapters & Guilds," Crisp's Blog, October 2012.

Henrik Kniberg, "Spotify Engineering Culture, Part 1 (a.k.a. the 'Spotify Model')," YouTube, 30 July 2019. www.youtube.com/watch?v=Yvfz4HGtoPc

Integrative Decision-Making
Loomio Help, "Consent process," help.loomio.com/en/guides/consent_process/index.html

Psychological Safety
Mikael Krogerus interview with Amy Edmondson, 10 November 2021.

Amy Edmondson, "Psychological Safety and Learning Behavior in Work Teams," *Administrative Science Quarterly* 44:2, 1999

The Ladder of Inference
Peter M. Senge, *The Fifth Discipline: The Art and Practice of the Learning Organisation* (London: Random House Business, 2006).

Assume Positive Intent
Katie Sola, "20 Business Magnates Share the Wisdom They Learned from Their Fathers," Forbes, 14 June 2016.

The Bad Apple Experiment
Will Felps, Terence Mitchell and Eliza Byington, "How, When, and Why Bad Apples Spoil the Barrel: Negative Group Members and Dysfunctional Groups," *Research in Organizational Behavior* 27:3, 2006.

The Reciprocity Ring
Wayne Baker, "The Paying It Forward Paradox," TEDx Talk, YouTube, 19 April 2016. www.youtube.com/watch?v=PwfSvQkeRXA

Radical Candor
Kim Scott, *Radical Candor: How to Get What You Want by Saying What You Mean* (London: Pan Macmillan, 2019).

4-in-1 Perspective
Frigga Haug, "The 'Four-in-One Perspective': A Manifesto for a More Just Life," *Socialism and Democracy* 23:1, 2009.

Burnout
Conversation with Benno Maggi, 8 October 2021.

Small Wins
Karl Weick, "Small Wins: Redefining the Scale of Social Problems," *American Psychologist* 39:1, 1984.

Tools of Cooperation
Clayton M. Christensen, Matt Marx and Howard H. Stevenson, "The Tools of Cooperation and Change," *Harvard Business Review*, October 2006.

Servant Leadership
Robert Greenleaf, "The Servant as Leader," in W. C. Zimmerli, M. Holzinger and K. Richter (eds), *Corporate Ethics and Corporate Governance* (Berlin and Heidelberg: Springer, 2007).

Reorg
Internal talk by Marc Werner given at Galenica AG.

The Premortem
Gary Klein, "Performing a Project Premortem," *Harvard Business Review*, September 2007.

The Postmortem
Henrik Kniberg, "Spotify Engineering Culture, Part 1 (a.k.a. the 'Spotify Model')," YouTube, 30 July 2019. www.youtube.com/watch?v=Yvfz4HGtoPc

Consensus versus Consent
Christian Rüther, *Soziokratie, S3, Holakratie, Frederic Laloux' "Reinventing Organizations" und "New Work"* (Books on Demand, 2018).

Two Workers, Two Levels
Dag Grødal, "Hvem lager murstein og hvem bygger katedral? Om prosjekters formål og håndtering av interessenter" ("Who lays the bricks and who builds a cathedral? On the purpose of a project and how to handle stakeholders"), thesis delivered at BI Norwegian Business School, Oslo Campus, 2017.

Purpose
Andreas Diehl, "Purpose – Führung ohne Anführer?" ("Purpose: Leadership without a Leader"), Digitale Neuordnung, 11 May 2021.

North Star Metrics
We were unable to determine who originally came up with the North Star Metric. Most sources refer to Sean Ellis, the concept's most enthusiastic proponent these days – but the concept is no doubt an old one.

Sean Ellis, "Finding the Right North Star Metric," Growth Hackers, 16 April 2019.

Saying Yes
We were unable to find a properly formulated theory for this one, and instead drew on many of our personal experiences.

Saying No
If you want to find out more about saying no, we recommend Greg McKeown's *Essentialism: The Disciplined Pursuit of Less* (London: Ebury, 2014). It's probably the smartest thing that has been written on the subject.

Corporate Culture
Merve Emre, "The Repressive Politics of Emotional Intelligence," *New Yorker*, 12 April 2021.

Team Culture
Francesca Gino and Jeffrey Huizinga, "Steve Kerr: Coaching the Golden State Warriors to Joy, Compassion, Competition, and Mindfulness," *Harvard Business School Case Collection*, July 2020.

You can listen to Steve Kerr talking to Pete Carroll about his coaching strategy in this excellent Ringer podcast (13 April 2020): theringer. com/2020/4/13/21218869/ flying-coach-with-steve-kerr-petecarroll-two-champions-mentors-philosophies-why-they-coach-premiere

The Trust Triangle
Frances Frei and Anne Morriss, *Unleashed: The Unapologetic Leader's Guide to Empowering Everyone Around You* (Boston, MA: Harvard Business Review Press, 2020).

Sutton's Good and Bad Bosses
Robert I. Sutton, *Good Boss, Bad Boss: How to Be the Best … and Learn from the Worst* (London: Piatkus, 2010).

Robert I. Sutton, "Are You in Tune with Your People or Living in a Fool's Paradise? Three Diagnostic Questions for Every Boss," Bob Sutton Work Matters, 20 August 2010.

Building a Team
Daniel Coyle, *The Culture Code: The Secrets of Highly Successful Groups* (New York: Random House, 2018).

The XY Theory
Douglas McGregor, *The Human Side of Enterprise* (New York: McGraw-Hill, 1960).

Diversity
David Rock and Paulette Gerkovich, "Why Diverse Teams Outperform Homogeneous Teams," NeuroLeadership Institute, 10 June 2021.

Performance versus Trust
Mike Knight, Simon Sinek: "Performance vs Trust," YouTube, 10 November 2019. www.youtube.com/watch?v=kJdXjtSnZTI

Lift-Out
J. Richard Hackman, *Leading Teams: Setting the Stage for Great Performances – The Five Keys to Successful Teams* (Boston, MA: Harvard Business School Press, 2002).

Robert S. Huckman and Gary P. Pisano, "The Firm Specificity of Individual Performance: Evidence from Cardiac Surgery," *Management Science* 52:4, 2006.

Flat Hierarchies
Gareth Morgan, *Images of Organization* (Thousand Oaks, CA: Sage, 2006).

Sociocracy
Bernhard Bockelbrink, James Priest and Liliana David, "A Practical Guide for Evolving Agile and Resilient Organizations with Sociocracy 3.0," S3.

Frederic Laloux, *Reinventing Organizations: An Illustrated Invitation to Join the Conversation on Next-Stage Organizations* (Fownhope, UK: Nelson Parker, 2016).

Nunchi
Euny Hong, *The Power of Nunchi: The Korean Secret to Happiness and Success* (London: Hutchinson, 2019).

ABOUT THE AUTHORS

Mikael Krogerus is Finnish, but was born in Stockholm and studied at the Kaospilot business school in Denmark. After graduating, he worked for the *Neue Zürcher Zeitung*'s *Folio* supplement, among others. Today, he is editor at *Das Magazin* in Zurich and enjoys cross-country skiing (preferably in a group).

Roman Tschäppeler is Swiss, was born in Bern, and also studied at Kaospilot. He also has an MA from the Zurich University of the Arts. Through his guzo.ch studio, he gives advice on strategy and creative matters, and he enjoys playing tennis (with a preference for singles).

They are the authors of the internationally bestselling series "Little Books for Big Questions," which includes *The Decision Book*, *The Change Book*, *The Test Book*, *The Question Book* and *To Do*. Their books have been translated into more than twenty-five languages and have sold millions of copies.

www.rtmk.ch

ACKNOWLEDGMENTS

It is the nature of the beast that you can't write a book about working with others alone. Our thanks to our backstage dream team:

Simon Brunner for his quick ideas and cheerfulness; Louisa Dunnigan, Emily Frisella, Philippa Logan and Patrick Taylor at Profile Books; Ruben Feurer & Flurin Hess for elaborating #newwork and #decisionmaking; Marc & Christian Gehri for allowing us to observe what it's like when two brothers manage a company; Alain Gloor for giving us an insight into how teams find each other; Till Grünewald & Nadine Inhelder for trusting Roman enough to develop a new master plan with him; Dag Grødal for reality-checking the topics and for his inspiration; the Kaospilot School for being 20 years ahead of its time; the wonderful team at Kein & Aber, our publishing home for the past 14 years, especially Johanna von Rauch, Ulle Bourceau, Muriel Pérez, Ann-Kristin Müller, Ulrike Groeger, Maurice Ettlin & Peter Haag; J. D. Kemming, for your inspiration and help in thinking things through; Kevin & Katrin Kunz, for giving us access to your change process; Fabrizio Laneve, for your enthusiasm and support; Benno Maggi, for our solution-oriented sparring sessions; Ondine Riesen for paving the way for #newwork; Franziska Schutzbach for everything; the entire team at "Tagi-Magi," who tolerate our ideas week after week, and frequently ennoble them; Roger Tinner for his eagle-eyed reading and congeniality; Hans Traffelet for his intelligence and sensitivity; and Marc Werner for his eye-opening introduction to servant leadership.